Contents

INDEX ON CENSORSHIP
VOLUME 42 NUMBER 04

Supported using public funding by

ARTS COUNCIL
ENGLAND

A historic tale of religious freedom and free speech

by **Rachael Jolley**

EDITORIAL

42(4): 3/5 | DOI: 10.1177/0306422013515109

IN CENTURIES PAST, citizens of many countries were thrown into jail for not conforming with the state religion; or for choosing to worship in a way unapproved by their rulers.

Today, some still are.

In centuries past, questioning religious belief was considered heresy; people were afraid to discuss and debate issues with a religious dimension; those who practised non-conformist religions were ostracised and were banned from holding government or other official posts.

Today, to question a religious "truth" or practice can still bring dire consequences; to choose to practise a religion alternative to the accepted or mainstream faith can still mean being beaten, purged, or suffering extreme discrimination.

The freedom to choose what we believe and how we practise our beliefs, and the counterbalancing freedom to discuss and question those beliefs: these are basic freedoms, but they are often not upheld.

There is another, more hidden, threat to freedom. Those who worry about offending another's religious beliefs in speech, writing or action may practise self-censorship to a level at which they stop themselves tackling a subject. They may constrain their own freedom to question or to challenge from fear of offending those who argue that religious customs must be exempt from question.

History contains many examples of how the state uses accusations of blasphemy to attack its opponents, and critics, and to defend its hierarchy. From Daniel Defoe to Martin Luther to the Scopes "Monkey" Trial, the idea that individuals who argue for change have somehow taken a stand against God has been used to undermine their actions, and make their supporters afraid. So when new "blasphemy" laws are introduced, as they have been recently in Russia, commentators are wary that its purpose is to give extra clout to the Russian government's existing crackdowns on authors and artists.

Fighters for religious tolerance have usually been defenders of free speech. John Milton, for one, spoke out for freedom of religious choice, and for the right to question, for "the liberty to know, to utter, and to argue according to conscience above all liberties; truth is strong next to the Almighty, she needs no policies, no stratagems, no licensing to make her victorious". Oxford University, horrified by such views, had Milton's books burnt in 1683, but the strength of his words lives on to stimulate the idea of freedom of speech and freedom of religion as basic rights. It should be remembered that he wrote at a time when those who practised non-conformist religions – Methodists, Quakers and Ranters →

Credit: Patrick De Noirmont/Reuters

ABOVE: An Afghan demonstrator counts his prayer beads as he marches through the streets of the Afghan capital of Kabul

→ among them – were, for religious reasons, not accepted at Oxford and Cambridge universities. Writers such as Defoe, Bunyan and Milton, who spoke up for dissenters, wrote some of their most famous words about freedoms when they faced adversity, and in prison.

Their words will resonate with writers of today who struggle against adversity and threat, and use their pens to work for greater freedoms. Their arguments for justice for those who challenge authority, government and mainstream shibboleths would be recognised by award-winning Belarus journalist Iryna Khalip, who is profiled in this issue by fellow Belarusian journalist Andrei Aliaksandrau. Many things change, and many challenges stay the same.

In this special report we look at all angles of these freedoms, from religion and offence to freedom of expression; from those who are banned from practising their religion to those who use religion to stop others from expressing their worries, thoughts or words.

In every corner of the world, there are questions about religion and freedom; and it is likely to be a moot subject for the rest of the century. Every country has its own issues, as well as those that cross over borders and boundaries, about religious freedom and freedom to discuss religion; about the lines between belief and freedoms. Through the centuries religion has been used as an instrument to crack down on practices, attitudes or people that the government would like to repress; in other words, to ensure conformity.

Some governments still operate at that level. In this issue, Alexander Verkhovsky discusses the new "blasphemy" law in Russia and its implications, as well as recent incidents where the government has banned art works or speech because religious offence may be caused or perceived. In China the Uighur Muslims have been terrorised by a campaign that stigmatises them as terrorists, and does not allow them to live as other citizens do.

For centuries small religious groups have been persecuted by larger ones, leading to mass immigration in search of a better, freer life. To some setting up new post-revolution states, such as India and the United States, the answer was a secular state where church and state were separated. In both those countries, the cornerstone of secular separation is under challenge. In the US, state boards of education want more powers to edit the content of school textbooks in line with particular religious views, and in India we see the rise of a strain of Hindu nationalism, which tries to place Hinduism above other religions in Indian society.

Is there a subject that a comedian or satirist should stop him or herself addressing? Are some religions more off limits than others? Should we worry about religious offence? Martin Rowson takes on this complex subject with his customary humour in words and cartoons.

And in her article for this issue, Samira Ahmed considers why liberals in democracies are so nervous about offending someone's culture or religion and whether they shy away from criticising policies or practices that are unlawful or unacceptable.

Looking back across the centuries, we might learn from what has happened in the past, and realise that we should be better prepared for the next attempt to curtail our freedoms and liberties. John Stuart Mill puts the point well when he argues that in silencing an opinion we rob the human race; in debating it, we learn either of its truth or of its errors. ☒

©Rachael Jolley
www.indexoncensorship.org

Rachael Jolley is editor of Index on Censorship

***In November Index on Censorship was awarded the prestigious Hermann Kesten prize by German PEN for outstanding efforts in support of persecuted writers. The award was presented by Belarus journalist Iryna Khalip*

ABOVE: Patriarch of Moscow leads a call to prayer at the Orthodox Church at the Christ the Saviour Cathedral, Moscow.

SPECIAL REPORT

In this section

Sound and fury

42(4): 8/11 | DOI: 10.1177/0306422013512590

Bishop of Bradford **Nick Baines** discusses persecution of Christians in Sudan by a leader who believes in one religion and one language for all, as well as moves to suppress minority voices

FREEDOM OF EXPRESSION is of universal importance, but its absence is sometimes more easily seen through the lens of a different culture. The familiar landscape of "home" can sometimes hinder a proper appreciation of the absence of freedoms, being outside of one's comfort zone can heighten awareness of reality. In this article I want to approach the matter from the outside in.

Early in 2013 I visited Sudan for the first time. The diocese of Bradford has had a partnership with Sudan for 30 years, and I was linked for a decade with Anglican dioceses in Zimbabwe (in my previous post as Bishop of Croydon). I thought I could easily switch attention from one African country to another. The reality was different.

Zimbabwe is ruled by Robert Mugabe, a man so corrupt that even his own demise will not clear the path to a golden new age – there are too many people who need to be protected by power well into the future. Sudan is governed by Omar al Bashir, a man committed to the project of creating a single nation (Sudan) with a single ethnicity (Arab), a single language (Arabic) and a single religion (Islam). There is a degree of shameful incompetence about Mugabe's manipulation of power and the consequent destruction of the Zimbabwean economy and the country's political culture. But al Bashir knows exactly what he is doing. And he does it in the face of a serious indictment by the International Criminal Court (ICC) for genocide in Darfur: he feels untouchable.

Since 99 per cent of southerners voted in 2011 for the division of Sudan into two independent states, Sudan and South Sudan, al Bashir has chosen to make the secessionists take responsibility for their choice – to some extent understandably. If they are so keen on having their own country, then they can go there... and then apply for visas to come to Sudan as foreigners. Harsh? Yes, but he could be seen to be compelling the South Sudanese to live with the consequences of their actions. Democratic choices bring consequences.

However, the real experience of this is the expulsion from Sudan of anyone deemed to originate in the south – even several generations ago. Those who remain – often because they are married to Sudanese – are prohibited from working. Apart from the human cost of this policy, the effect on the Anglican church (the Episcopal Church of Sudan, which has not divided along with the states) is an exodus of leaders, an increased dependency of those who remain on the goodwill and generosity of other Sudanese Christians. And this is happening alongside

ABOVE: A South Sudanese worshipper arrives to attend Sunday prayers in Baraka Parish church at Hajj Yusuf, Khartoum

massive population migration in the wake of the ongoing genocide in Darfur, government violence in South Kordofan and Blue Nile state. Khartoum has had to absorb destitute migrants on an unimaginable scale.

Those displaced are almost exclusively African. They speak African languages (derogatorily referred to as "twittering" by the Arabs). They are mostly (but not exclusively) Christian.

My visit to Khartoum earlier this year ended when my wife and I left a Christian-owned guesthouse at 1am in order to get to the airport for the flight back to →

→ Manchester. Within an hour the guesthouse had been raided by the security services, all property confiscated, and all residents and guests taken in for questioning. Foreign guests were deported and the family that ran the guesthouse was removed; the father of the family is now prohibited from working. This might not sound too dramatic – especially in the light of reports from parts of the Middle East and South Asia where Christians are being targeted for violence or forced to convert to Islam – but it comes as part of a deliberate policy on the part of government to exclude Christians and force them to leave for the South. This necessarily puts pressure on Christians to keep quiet, but the bishops (in particular) continue to be unafraid to engage courageously with "the powers".

It seems that al Bashir blames the international community for refusing to welcome him back into the fold by removing the ICC indictment after the peaceful transition to two states. Foreigners are to be removed, even when they provide essential services that cannot be provided locally. We met European medical personnel who had spent their working lives developing medical facilities in local communities, and who now found themselves thrown out, leaving medical provision severely weakened.

Why destroy social, educational and medical infrastructure simply in order to save face? Riots in September 2013 in Khartoum (initially about the removal of fuel subsidies) demonstrated that economic matters do not always serve the interests of the government of the day.

But there is a bigger question relevant beyond Sudan. How do we understand and clearly define the categories in which and through which we see political, religious and cultural phenomena? Getting the category wrong leads inevitably to miscomprehension, to a potentially dangerous misapplication of rhetoric/language... and this has political consequences.

My own diocese of Bradford has a high percentage of Muslims from south Asia. Immigration began in the mid-20th century in order to staff the textile mills of West Yorkshire. Many of Bradford's Muslims originate from the region of Kashmiri Mirpur in Pakistan. This concentration necessarily affects how the community lives and organises in Bradford, how it is influenced by (and, in turn, influences) events back in Pakistan, and how it is understood by the non-Pakistani population in the city.

One of the first lessons I had to learn when I came to Bradford nearly three years ago was not to confuse ethnicity with religion. What might appear to be a phenomenon rooted in religious identity (certain modes of dress, for example) might actually be more appropriately understood as a cultural phenomenon that coincidentally becomes associated with religious identity. To confuse the two can be dangerous. What I have in mind here is where violence (in particular) is attributed to religion, when religious tagging is clearly a tribal badging designed to hide more cultural (or other) identity.

Examples of this can be seen in the Northern Ireland of the Troubles or the sectarian destructiveness of Lebanon. Although the categories cannot easily be extricated from one another, at least those who observe or comment on such events should have the intelligence to dig a little deeper into the categorisation of such phenomena before simplistically eliding culture and religion as if they were synonymous.

The point is that there are two dangers here: (a) that category errors lead to poor communication and confusion, and (b) that people might be reluctant to speak out on serious matters simply because they fear being accused of racism or simply getting it wrong. This doesn't help anyone where honest and frank conversation is needed and mutual critique is essential to good relationships.

This takes us back to Sudan. It is not a simple matter – capable of easy explication

or distinction – to work out what can be attributed to which category. Al Bashir's policy seems clearly to create a political, ethnic, religious and cultural identity in which there is no place for diversity. One can assume that he is aiming at a myth of solidarity – that if everyone claims the same identity, they will buy into the same projects, have the same friends and enemies, defend the same categories and communicate in the same way. Of course, this fails to take into account the complex reality of human identity construction and how complex and diverse people interrelate and self-identify.

In one sense all this should not need to be articulated. If Muslim is blowing up Muslim in Pakistan or Afghanistan, then there is clearly more going on than mere "religion" or religious identity. Simply reporting atrocities as if they were political or cultural events (without reference to religious allegiance) is as naïve as to report on religion without reference to the ethnic, political, economic, social or cultural identities that shape religious expression.

This is not a plea for obfuscation or mitigation of religiously motivated violence. On the contrary, it is a plea for the sort of literacy that seeks to comprehend in order to know how to think about and respond to phenomena that might all-too-easily be capable of simplistic categorisation.

Language goes to the heart of this. Not only the language of explanation or reportage, but the ways in which language is (or particular languages are) seen to be totems of identities that are deemed to be inconvenient. In Zimbabwe identity is tied up inextricably with language: the Shona-speaking government has demonstrated in past violence what it thinks of the Ndebele-speaking Matabele. In Sudan African languages – mostly spoken by Christians of African (rather than Arabic) origin – are being derided and squeezed out. This is one reason why some churches in Sudan put such high value on keeping their own languages alive, teaching them to both children and adults, working hard (with pitiful resources) to reserve their means of communication as an integral element of cultural and religious identity. Language is as much part of individual and common identity as is skin colour, and nobody should be compelled to lose their native tongue.

One of the most penetrating verses of the Old Testament is found in the book of Proverbs. Seized upon by opponents of Hitler during the 1930s and 1940s in Germany, it demands that we "open our mouths for the dumb" – that is, that those who have a voice must keep alive the songs and lan-

Language is as much part of individual and common identity as skin colour

guage of people whose voice is silenced by the exercise of corrupt power. The moral demands of this are clear here also. But, for that voice to be heard and understood, it is essential that intelligent consideration is given to ensuring that the categories of speech and identification are kept as accurate as possible.

Responding to religious phenomena as if they were merely "cultural" is as dangerous and misplaced as eliding all cultural phenomena as merely "religious" – and runs the risk of stopping people speaking truthfully and accurately when religion is the root of violence or cultural violence seeks to hide behind a religious facade. The world is more complex than that. We can and must do better. ⊠

©Nick Baines
www.indexoncensorship.org

The Right Reverend **Nicholas Baines** is the Bishop of Bradford.

Cape God

42(4): 12/17 | DOI: 10.1177/0306422013511762

Natasha Joseph interviews the chairman of the African Christian Democratic Party about her views on South African politics, religion and conservative values

SOUTH AFRICA IS, at once, a deeply religious country and one whose relationship with organised religion – particularly Christianity – is inextricably entangled with its apartheid history. The National Party, which ruled from 1948 until 1994, considered itself a Christian organisation – one which found unwavering support for its racist and divisive politics within the then-powerful Dutch Reformed Church. Hendrik Verwoerd, who served as prime minister from 1958 until he was assassinated in 1966, and is largely considered to be the architect of the apartheid system, studied theology when he first went to university. Biblical verses were used to justify the government's policies of separate development.

Then came 1994, and with it the advent of democracy in South Africa. The country was no longer to be guided by, among other things, dangerous misreadings of the Bible – instead, the constitution became the cornerstone of all South African law and, in many ways, its moral compass. It is prefaced by the bill of rights, which enshrines freedom of religion, sexual orientation, culture and criminalises discrimination on these or other grounds such as gender and race.

There have been only a few high-profile fierce "moral" battles between the country's more conservative religious and cultural groupings and those who live by the constitution's more liberal interpretation of citizens' rights and responsibilities. Chief among these have been bruising public fights around same-sex marriages (South Africa is the only country on the African continent that not only allows these unions but does not criminalise the act of homosexuality), abortion and corporal punishment. There is another battle on the horizon: the country's Minister of Social Development Bathabile Dlamini announced in July that a new law, currently in the drafting stages, would make it illegal for parents to spank their children at home. Dlamini was quoted in the Sunday Times as saying: "If a husband beats a wife it's a crime, but if a parent hits a child who is helpless, it's not illegal." The newspaper reported that, under the draft law, parents would be charged with assault if, at home, they used a flat hand on a child's bottom or applied any other form of corporal punishment.

It's useful, here, to consider South Africa's religious landscape nearly 20 years after Nelson Mandela became the country's first black and democratically elected president. There are two sources of information for quantifying how many South Africans consider themselves as belonging to religious groupings or who identify according to their religious beliefs: the 2001 census data, and the most recent WIN-Gallup International

ABOVE: Archbishop Desmond Tutu beside a statue of himself in Cape Town

Religiosity and Atheism Index, an international survey conducted between November 2011 and January 2012. The 2011 census did not feature any questions about religion, and Statistics South Africa – which carries out the census – explained itself thus at the time:

"In 2008, Stats SA embarked on a series of user consultations, to get advice as to what questions should be asked in the questionnaire. The question on religion was low on the list of priorities as informed by the users of census data, and it therefore did not make it onto the final list of data items." →

ABOVE: Members of the Shembe Church kneeling in water on the beach in Durban

→ (From the Census 2011 website: http://www.statssa.gov.za/census2011/faq.asp)

In 2001, Christianity in its many forms was by far the largest religious grouping. Of this, the largest denomination, by far, was the Zion Christian Church, or ZCC, a massive

She believes there is plenty of room for a political party like hers on the South African landscape despite the country's core values being contained in the constitution rather than any religious text

organisation which at the time counted more than three million people among its adherents. The ZCC and other neo-Pentecostal or charismatic churches, particularly those which mostly draw their members from black African communities across South Africa and elsewhere on the continent, have grown exponentially in the past 20 years. Recent, though unsubstantiated, estimates put the ZCC's membership alone at six million people.

Also in 2001, the Dutch Reformed Church – a spiritual home to mostly white, Afrikaans-speaking South Africans, the Catholic Church and Methodist churches were the country's largest religious groupings. Just 75,549 Jews and 654,064 Muslims were counted during the 2001 Census. In 2001, 79.77 per cent of South Africa's citizens identified themselves as religious in some way. By 2007, according to the website Religious Intelligence (www.religiousintelligence.com), that figure had dipped to 73.52 per cent of the population. The WIN-Gallup Index, released in August 2012, revealed that just 64 per cent of South Africans considered themselves religious or belonging to a religious group.

Despite the decline, Jo-Ann Downs believes that South Africa remains "deeply religious". Downs is the national chairman of the African Christian Democratic Party (ACDP), which is the largest

political party in the country whose values are based on a religion. Downs says they have between 30,000 and 40,000 members, and during the 2009 national elections the party secured three seats in South Africa's National Assembly. They also hold single seats in three provinces: the Western Cape, KwaZulu-Natal and Gauteng. Downs is quick to point out that while part of the party's identity – and its name – is "Christian", along with the associated Biblical values and beliefs, "we are much broader based". "In another country we'd be called conservative - – so, socially conservative, economically conservative,"she explained. There is, she believes, plenty of room for a political party like hers on the South African landscape despite the country's core values being contained in the constitution rather than any religious text. And she insists the ACDP and its members do not support censorship if it limits other people's rights. On the thorny issues of gay marriage and abortion, for instance: "On moral issues – we're pro-life. We don't want gay marriage to be forced on churches, or a situation where faith-based organisations can't say where they stand or 'This is what we believe'."

The Termination of Pregnancy (TOP) Act 92 of 1996 legalised abortion in South Africa (beginning on 1 February 1997) in the face of fierce religious opposition both in Parliament and on the streets. The Abortion and Sterilisation Act 2 of 1975, which the TOP replaced, allowed abortion only in specific circumstances: pregnancy had to seriously threaten a woman's physical or mental health; the unborn child had to be suffering physical or mental defects; or the pregnancy had to be the result of rape or incest. But the TOP changed this dramatically, stipulating – as the Reproductive Rights Alliance describes it – that "all women, irrespective of age, location or socio-economic status, can choose to terminate pregnancy without requiring the permission of their partners or

parents". The ACDP's members in parliament voted against the act.

This is a scenario in which religious beliefs and the law of the land collided loudly and publicly. The act criminalises anyone who "prevents the lawful termination of a pregnancy or obstructs access to a facility for the termination of pregnancy". But nurses and doctors who identify as religious and "pro-life" insisted that they should be exempt from performing abortions because the procedure fundamentally clashes with these beliefs. When the 1975 Act was repealed, the "conscience clause" – which allowed this exemption – was struck down, too. "Lots of doctors are pro-life," Downs said. "As part of a democracy, people have the right [to have these beliefs]. To them [performing an abortion] is being forced to murder." There have been many reported cases of nurses turning women away when they seek abortions at state facilities, and

This is a scenario in which religious beliefs and the law of the land collided loudly and publicly

using religiously charged ideals and values to decry those who choose abortion as an option. But, Downs says, it's important that while doctors or nurses are allowed to be conscientious objectors, they must not turn people away entirely, as this is in defiance of the country's laws. She says women must be referred to other clinicians who are morally willing to perform abortions, so that both parties' rights and beliefs are protected. The legislation has been tweaked to allow doctors or nurses to conscientiously object to performing abortions – but only if, as Downs suggests, they refer the woman in question to another practitioner. If no other practitioner is available and it is a →

→ medical emergency, the woman's rights override the practitioner's objections.

In 2006, South Africa legalised same-sex marriage – another law which is in line with the country's constitution but was angrily and emotionally rejected by its religious citizens and groups. Here, again, the ACDP says religious organisations shouldn't get a special exemption: they should, however, be given the option of refusing to marry a same-sex couple because to do so would clash directly with their faith. "The ACDP doesn't want to be in people's bedrooms," she said. In short, she argues, what people do in their own homes is neither her, the party nor religious groups' business – but churches shouldn't be forced to perform ceremonies at odds with their beliefs, much as nurses shouldn't be forced to perform abortions and have their right to belief and faith trodden on by somebody else's right to reproductive freedom.

Downs says the ACDP will support censorship in some – undefined – cases because "you can take liberalism too far". She cites the example of a Dutch political party, the Brotherly Love, Freedom and Diversity party, which contested the 2006 elections in the Netherlands. Among its policies? Cutting the age of sexual consent from 16 to 12 and legalising child pornography. It was disbanded in 2010 after failing to collect the 600 signatures required for participation in the national elections.

She thinks for a long time when asked what the next fight of this nature will be, then refers to what's been nicknamed "the smacking law". No date has yet been set for public hearings on and parliamentary discussion about the law, but the lines are appearing faintly in the sand. Already, children's rights groups – pointing to the Constitution and the Children's Act – are supporting the legislation, saying it's an important step to protect children. But the ACDP intends to oppose it, and Cape Town's Family Policy Institute, a Christian organisation, told newspaper the Cape Argus that getting the government involved in family matters could be dangerous. "The family itself is a unit and the government does not have the right to interfere with parental issues. How will criminalising parents decrease child abuse?" Errol Naidoo, the founder and president of the Family Policy Institute was quoted as saying.

It's a sentiment Downs echoes: in much the same way that her party doesn't want to enter people's bedrooms, it doesn't believe the government should intrude in people's homes.

It is a system that seems, for now, to be working in South Africa: no single religious grouping is more powerful at the ballot box than another, and the constitution remains a founding document which – while it may not always enjoy all citizens' support, is well respected and provides a good backbone for an ever-changing, often turbulent young democracy. X

©Natasha Joseph
www.indexoncensorship.org

Natasha Joseph is a journalist based in South Africa

Census 2001

Denomination	Adherents
Dutch Reformed churches	3,005,697
Zion Christian churches	4,971,931
Catholic churches	3,181,332
Methodist churches	3,035,719
Pentecostal/Charismatic churches	3,695,211
Anglican churches	1,722,076
Apostolic Faith Mission	246,193
Lutheran churches	1,130,983
Presbyterian churches	832,497
Bandla Lama Nazaretha	248,825
Baptist churches	691,235
Congregational churches	508,826
Orthodox churches	42,253
Other Apostolic churches	5,627,320
Other Zionist churches	1,887,147
Ethiopian type churches	1,150,102
Other Reformed churches	226,499
Other African independent churches	656,644
Other Christian churches	2,890,151
African traditional belief	125,898
Judaism	75,549
Hinduism	551,668
Islam	654,064
Other beliefs	283,815
No religion	6,767,165
Undetermined	610,974

Source: South Africa census 2001

A good book will keep you fascinated for days. A good bookshop for your whole life.

Waterstones

Defending the right
to be offended

42(4): 19/24 | DOI: 10.1177/0306422013512588

Freedom of expression must trump the commitment to tiptoe around some people's idea of multiculturalism, argues **Samira Ahmed**, looking back at the last 15 years

N **1999, THE** neo-Nazi militant David Copeland planted three nail bombs in London – in Brixton, Brick Lane and Soho – targeting black people, Bangladeshi Muslims and gays and lesbians. Three people died and scores were injured.

In response, the government awarded funds to local charities and community groups working on projects to build cohesion among the people that had been the targets of Copeland's bloody campaign.

The intention was honorable, the impact underwhelming. According to Angela Mason, then head of Stonewall, the gay rights pressure group, the assumption was that all the people targeted by Copeland were "on the same side". The truth as she sees it was that the government-funded projects exposed the uncomfortable reality that there were strong anti-gay prejudices among Muslim, Christian and black communities in Britain.

How realistic is it to expect a cohesive society could emerge from this kind of climate?

Today, the tensions between freedom of speech and religious belief remain acute – and they are systematically exploited by political groups of all stripes, from the English Defence League to radical Islamists who

threaten to disrupt the repatriation of dead British soldiers at Wootton Bassett. The story consistently makes the headlines. The idea that there is an Islamist assault on British freedoms and values is widespread.

The Muslim campaign against Salman Rushdie's The Satanic Verses in 1988 was the crucial moment in all this. It forced writers and artists from an Asian or Muslim background, whether they defined themselves that way or not, to take sides. They had to declare loyalty – or otherwise – to the offended.

The results have been appalling, and not only in Britain. Most notoriously, the Somali writer and Dutch politician Ayaan Hirsi Ali had her citizenship withdrawn by the Dutch authorities just as Muslim expressions of outrage and death threats in response to her writing about Islam reached their peak.

In the UK, local authorities have been all too ready to cave in to pressure under cover of preventing community unrest, maintaining public order or resisting perceived cultural insensitivity.

Sensitivity to religious insult, too often conflated with racism, has frequently taken precedence over concern for free →

ABOVE: Demonstration at Lowe's home improvement store by a interfaith group, Allen Park, Michigan. The chainstore bowed to pressure from the Florida Family Association and withdrew funding for the reality TV programme All-American Muslim

Credit: Jim West/Alamy

→ expression. In 2004 violent protests by Birmingham Sikhs led to the closure of Behzti, Gurpreet Kaur Bhatti's play on rape and abuse of women in a Sikh temple.

But the problem is not always obvious. In September 2012, Jasvinder Sanghera, founder of Karma Nirvana, a charity campaigning against forced marriage, ran a stall at the National Union of Teachers conference, distributing posters for schools. She told the Rationalist Association: "Many teachers came to my stall and many said, 'Well, we couldn't put them up. It's cultural,

we wouldn't want to offend communities and we wouldn't get support from the headteacher.' And that was the majority view of over 100 teachers who came to speak to me."

Sanghera said that one teacher who did take a poster sent her photographs of it displayed on a noticeboard in his school. But "within 24 hours of him putting up the posters, the headteacher tore them all down". The teacher was summoned to the head's office and told: "Under no circumstances must you ever display those posters again because we don't want to upset our Muslim parents."

The delayed prosecution of predominantly Asian Muslim grooming gangs in Rochdale and Oxford has to be seen in the context of the long-standing local authority fear of causing offence. Women's rights, artistic free speech, even child protection have repeatedly been downgraded in order to avoid the accusation of racism or religious insult.

It's not as bad as it used to be, according to Peter Tatchell, whose organisation OutRage! promotes the rights of lesbian, gay, bisexual and transgender people and has campaigned against homophobic and misogynist comments by Islamic preachers and organisations. "Official attitudes are better in terms of defending free speech but still far from perfect," he says. However, he adds, "Police and prosecutors still sometimes take the view that causing offence is sufficient grounds for criminal action, especially where religious and racial sensitivities are involved."

The pressure isn't necessarily overt but individual writers say they are struggling to work out where the lines are being drawn.

Writer Yasmeen Khan's work ranges from making factual programmes, including documentaries for BBC Radio Four, to writing and performing comedy and drama. She says: "The pressure not to 'offend' has certainly increased over the past few years," though she adds that it has probably affected writers and performers outside a particular religion more than believers.

Being seen as a religious believer can be an advantage when it comes to commissioning or applying for grants, she says. "But the downside is that you're sometimes only viewed through that lens; you don't want to be seen as a 'Muslim writer' – you just want to be a writer. It can feel like you're being pigeon-holed by others, and that holds you back as being seen as 'mainstream'. I've seen that issue itself being used for comedy – I was part of an Edinburgh show for which we wrote a sketch about an Asian writer being asked to 'Muslim-up' her writing."

Luqman Ali runs the award-winning Khayaal Theatre company in Luton. It has built a strong critical reputation for its dramatic interpretation of classical Islamic literature. He dismisses the assertion that political correctness has shut down artistic freedom: "There would appear to be an entrenched institutional narrative that casts Muslims as problem people and Muslim artists as worthy only in so far as they are either prepared to lend credence to this narrative or are self-avowedly irreligious," he says. He contrasts what he sees as the "retrospective acceptance" of historic Islamic

Sensitivity to religious insult, too often conflated with racism, has frequently taken precedence over concern for free expression

art and literary texts in museum collections with "very little acceptance of contemporary Muslim cultural production, especially in the performing arts".

In 2011, the TLC channel in the US cancelled the reality TV series All American Muslim, a programme about a family in Michigan, after only one season. The cancellation followed a campaign by the Florida Family Association that was reminiscent of the UK group Christian Voice's campaign against Jerry Springer: The Opera in 2005. Lowe's, a national home-improvement chainstore and major advertiser, pulled out of sponsoring the show after the group claimed the series was "propaganda that riskily hides the Islamic agenda's clear and present danger to American liberties and traditional values".

Lowe's denied its decision was in response to the Florida Family Association campaign. But amid the hysteria generated, including protests outside Lowe's stores, ratings for the show plummeted. Many Americans decided not to watch it. As with Jerry Springer: →

भारतीय

**Make Film !
Make Money!
But not on
behalf of
Tamilian`s
sovereignty**

MADRAS CAFE

DIRECTED BY SHOOJIT SIRCAR

BAN ! BAN!

ABOVE: Indian Tamils and Bharatiya Janta Party (BJP) protest against Hindi film Madras Cafe, Mumbai, 22 August 2013. The film was also withdrawn from Cineworld and Odeon cinemas in the UK after pressure from Tamil campaigning groups

→ The Opera, a small group had created a momentum of outrage that led to a fatal atmosphere of threat and intimidation around a piece of mainstream – and until then, highly successful – entertainment. The Bollywood thriller Madras Café was withdrawn from Cineworld and Odeon cinemas in the UK and Tamil Nadu, India, after a campaign by Tamil groups who found it "offensive".

Veteran comedy writer John Lloyd, speaking at a British Film Institute event marking the 50th anniversary of the broadcast of the satirical news programme That Was The Week That Was in 2012, said there was now an obsession with "compliance" by tier after tier of broadcast managers, which he felt had suffocated satire. "Now," said Lloyd, "everyone's jibbering in fright if you do anything at all." He contrasted the current climate to his experience working for Not The Nine O' Clock News when, he said, he was "encouraged to provoke and challenge".

Writer and stand-up comedian Stewart Lee, who co-wrote Jerry Springer: The Opera, is currently working on a new series of his award-winning Comedy Vehicle for BBC Two. He believes a general uncertainty about British legislation on religious offence is affecting what gets produced: "It's all very confusing. I don't know what I am allowed to say. There is a culture of fear generally now in broadcasting. No one knows what they are allowed to do."

"In Edinburgh in August 2013, a (non-broadcast) show in a tent funded by the BBC at 9.30pm saw the BBC person running it pull a song by the gay musical comedy duo Jonny and the Baptists about laws concerning gays giving blood because it 'promoted homosexuality'. This at 9.30pm, in a country where it is not illegal to promote homosexuality, and not for broadcast.

"In series one of Comedy Vehicle, I had a bit on imagining Islamists training dogs to fly planes into buildings. This was pulled on the grounds that it appeared deliberately provocative to Muslims because of the dog taboo in Islam. I looked into this, and read a load of stuff on it. There is no dog taboo in the Muslim faith."

A BBC spokesman said: "The band were invited to perform on our open garden stage which was run as a family friendly venue for the 24 days it was open to the public. With the possibility of children and young people in the audience, we asked the band to tailor their short set to reflect the audience. They did so, and in one of these, a late night not-for-broadcast show, their set included the song which Stewart Lee refers to. The BBC has a strong track record of offering comedians opportunities to perform their edgiest material without restraint during the festival and we will continue to do so."

The pressure not to "offend" has certainly increased over the past few years

Lee described the Jerry Springer: The Opera debacle, explaining that the pressure group Christian Voice "were able to scupper the viability of the 2005-2006 tour" of the play by informing theatres they would be prosecuted under the forthcoming incitement to religious hatred bill if they staged the play. The bill was later defeated by one vote in the Commons, and soon after the House of Lords scrapped the blasphemy laws. "But," says Lee, "I think the public perception is that both these laws still exist."

He says he doesn't like to make a fuss: "The BBC is beset on all sides by politically and economically interested partners who want to see it destroyed. I wouldn't expect the BBC, any more, to go to the wall about something I wanted to say. I'd just say it somewhere else – on a long touring show for example – and get better paid for it anyway! I am also anxious not to appear to →

→ contribute to the notion that 'political correctness has gone mad'. People say, 'ah but you've never done stuff about Islam'. I have. Nothing happened. But I have not done stuff about Islam in the depth I have stuff about Christianity as it is not relevant to me in the same way."

Lee says his writing for tours isn't affected by the fear of offence because his solo tours are "cost-effective and largely off the radar of the anti-PC brigade or people looking for things to complain about".

However, he says, when it comes to the television series, he does consider the power of offence. "It affects what I write," he says. His new show addresses the Football Association's objection to the word "nigger". He suspects that the BBC might get cold feet about this bit. "So I will drop it and use it live and on DVD. I don't see TV as the place to experiment with certain types of content any more."

But he says that one of the most important things about freedom of speech is that it applies to everyone. "I don't think a lot of the jokes that, say, Jimmy Carr and Frankie Boyle do are worth the annoyance they cause, but I would defend their right to say them."

So what, if anything, has changed for writers and what they feel they can write about since his experience with Jerry Springer?

"It's all much worse," Lee says. "But for many reasons: lack of funding mainly." In April 2013, culture secretary Maria Miller addressed members of the arts industry at the British Museum, arguing that: "When times are tough and money is tight, our focus must be on culture's economic impact."

But as Lee points out, "it's harder to justify funding something worthwhile in the current climate if people are storming the publicly funded theatre, such as Behzti, in protest." "It has lost its moral authority in many ways," he says, adding that ratings are at the forefront of commissioners' minds.

There have been high-profile attempts to link comedy and Islam, such as the recent Allah Made Me Funny international standup tours. The Canadian CBC sitcom Little Mosque on the Prairie defied self-styled Muslim community leaders' complaints about insult and offence to run for six highly-rated seasons, finishing in 2012. The BBC's own Citizen Khan, which begins its second series in 2014, has similarly ignored claims of insult. Both sitcoms combine a Muslim family setting with very familiar sitcom themes.

In Britain, the overly cautious attitude to free speech and religion supposed to create community harmony has coincided with growing fundamentalist intimidation often promoted within enclosed immigrant communities. Sikh gangs have targeted mixed weddings in temples, and there have been tense stand-offs between Sikhs and Muslims over allegations of sexual grooming in Luton and elsewhere. British Ahmadiyya Muslims, who fled persecution in Pakistan, have struggled to draw media attention to the orchestrated hate campaigns being conducted against them by some Sunni groups. We need to feel free to criticise religious groups when they cross lines and commit crimes, without worrying about the cultural upset.

As Kenan Malik has said, the refusal to confront these issues in open and frank discussion, is "transforming the landscape" of free speech. Even in the United States, where free speech is enshrined in the constitution, there are serious questions being asked about what free speech actually means – particularly when it comes to religion.

The right to free speech should never be half-hearted. People have the right to be offended, but they don't have the right to stop others speaking, discussing and debating ideas. ⌧

© Samira Ahmed
www.indexoncensorship.org

Samira Ahmed is a broadcast journalist

Pressure points

42(4): 25/30 | DOI: 10.1177/0306422013513123

In Turkey,the Islamic media continues to face significant pressure. Journalist **Kaya Genç** assesses its position in society and examines its rapidly changing image, impact and future

ONE DAY IN 1997, a young journalist just starting out in her career, Nihal Bengisu Karaca, went to a concert given by the Red Army choir in Istanbul's Cemil Topuzlu concert hall.

Towards the end of the performance, the choir performed the Tenth Year March, a nationalist song written and composed in 1933 to celebrate the tenth anniversary of the foundation of Turkish republic.

At the time the march was frequently used to send a clear political message to certain sectors of Turkish society, namely the Kurds and the religious, that the country's actual hosts were nationalist and secular Turks. Others were merely guests in the country.

After the choir finished singing the audience rose to their feet and began applauding, at which point a woman approached Karaca and her friend, who both wore headscarves.

She told them that they had no right to applaud and that they didn't "deserve" the march. "In a normal society you expect the bourgeois class to be democratic and supportive of freedoms and plurality," Karaca says. "That night I realised this was not the case. Turkey's bourgeois class considers itself to be the country's aristocrats whose job it is to protect the oligarchic system at all costs." She describes people's reactions to headscarved women at the time as "hysterical". The same year, when Karaca politely asked a

man to stop talking during a film, he refused, dismissing her as a regressive individual, who had no right to enjoy the film, or even be in the cinema.

Karaca spent a lot of the 1990s in film theatres and concert halls for good reason. Her love of the arts was more than just a personal interest. It was professional, because she was a journalist writing about the arts. Karaca, now a columnist at the mainstream HaberTürk newspaper, started her career in the country's Islamic media. In the 1980s the Islamic media was under intense pressure from the state, the Turkish General Staff and a group of mainstream media organisations who saw them as a threat to the stability of the republic.

In Turkey, the media is divided into three main groups, the liberal-secular media with no religious affiliation or prejudices (Taraf, Radikal), the nationalist media with an anti-Islamist agenda (Hürriyet, Aydınlık, Vatan, Sözcü), and the Islamic media. The Islamic media includes two sub-branches: liberal-centre (Zaman, Star, Sabah) and conservative-rightwing Islamist (Yeni Şafak, Yeni Akit). Star and Yeni Şafak both sell more than 100,000 copies each. Yeni Akit sells more than 50,000 copies and Yeni Şafak more than 100,000.

Karaca's first job was at the weekly news magazine Aksiyon where she was the →

ABOVE: Journalists and activists participate in a rally calling for press freedom in Ankara

Credit: Umit Bektas/Reuters

→ only woman employee. She worked there as a reporter, editor and film critic. At the same time she was carrying on her studies at the university but her academic interests were almost stifled when the authorities forced her to remove her headscarf to be allowed to enter the exam hall. "I was crying while trying to answer the questions," she says. "If someone made me remove my veil on the street, it would no doubt be considered a crime or an act of abuse. But when the state did the same it became perfectly legal."

ABOVE: A demonstrator holds a banner during a protest against the constitutional court's verdict about headscarves at universities in Istanbul in 2008.

Things changed dramatically for Karaca and her colleagues in 1997 when the top brass of the Turkish military forced the country's elected prime minister and the leader of the Welfare Party, Necmettin Erbakan, to approve a number of legislative acts it had drafted in the headquarters of the Turkish General Staff in Ankara. That day, 28 February 1997, the day the generals forced the prime minister to sign the declaration, turned into a big embarrassment for Erbakan, who saw himself as the representative of the country's Islamist and conservative citizens. The memorandum included legislation that banned headscarves in universities and introduced extensive control over newspapers which didn't bow to the official discourse of the military.

"At the time 90 per cent of the media had the same political view with which they indoctrinated their readers," Karaca says. "And the media was extremely powerful: a media proprietor could harm or remove a government with a strong headline and →

pick members of the new government behind closed doors. They were always on good terms with the military high command and used this friendship to their advantage. If a government didn't comply with their views they threatened them with the 'coup card'."

The military memorandum of 1997, widely known in Turkey as the 'post-modern coup', is a case in point. Leading secular voices in the media had supported the coup, a handful of liberal columnists objected to it and most Islamists condemned it. The military rewarded the secularist media by giving their journalists lengthy interviews about the

More than three hundred generals successfully sued one Anadolu'da Vakit columnist for libel

military's political agenda which effectively replaced the discourse of elected politicians. They also gave extensive access to army facilities to journalists supportive of the military's intervention in the government of the country.

Alarmed by the developments and in fear for their safety, some Islamic publications backed down and changed the tone of their coverage. "After the postmodern coup our magazine decided to run a cover story about how Turkish Islamists did not want an Islamic state," Karaca remembers. "Some conservative and religious groups were forced to prove that they were not Islamists like members of the Welfare Party." Anadolu'da Vakit, the country's hardline Islamist paper did the opposite and ran angry denunciations of the military elite and their activities.

More than three hundred generals successfully sued one Anadolu'da Vakit columnist for libel and the proprietor of the paper was ordered to pay the unprecedented sum of two trillion Turkish liras in damages. The newspapers ceased its operations only to return a few years later under the new title, Yeni Akit.

"In the media we were greatly outnumbered by supporters of the coup," Karaca says. "That only a handful of people stood by us heartened the generals who announced that the 1997 coup would continue for a 'thousand years'."

Not only did the coup fail to last for a "thousand years" but it also became the subject of a massive trial in Turkey a mere sixteen years after the generals published their memorandum. The chief of staff and a group of generals accused of being behind the postmodern coup became defendants of the "February 28 trials'" There are currently 103 defendants being prosecuted, 36 of them are in custody. When the trial began in September this year, there were calls from Islamist columnists to 'extend' the range of the investigation and to go after media proprietors and opinion leaders supportive of the coup.

But however objectionable their views, prosecuting media bosses and journalists is extremely problematic for Turkey's AKP government. Over the course of the last year the government had been accused of stifling press freedoms and prosecuting dissident voices by the world's leading freedom of expression groups, including the Index on Censorship and the New York based Committee to Protect Journalists (CPJ).

According to Ferhat Ünlü, who also worked for an Islamist newspaper in 1997, the February 28 trial may have dangerous consequences. "It is not right to hang a Sword of Damocles over certain social, economic and political groups," he says. "Arresting journalists would only intensify Turkey's already intensified society." Ünlü agrees that the mainstream media did a regrettable job during the coup era but says the editors should pay "a professional price" for what they did rather than a legal one. He believes that the country's conservative media is repeating some of the mistakes the mainstream media made in the 1990s.

"Many people were subjected to character assassinations during the recent trials," he says, referring to the Sledgehammer and Ergenekon court cases where a number of military personnel and journalists were convicted of plotting a failed coup to overthrow the government. Ünlü, who now works as a columnist and editor for Sabah newspaper, says some journalists in today's new mainstream media will have a hard time in the future coping with the moral weight of recent events.

Ünlü started journalism in 1995 on the Islamist Yeni Şafak where he worked until 2004. He was then hired by Newsweek's Turkish edition. He specialises in state intelligence and security issues. An avid reader of John le Carré and Dostoyevsky, he is an author with four novels to his name. Ünlü remembers how he faced difficulties when he started as a reporter. "The doors of mainstream media were closed to journalism students like me who came to Istanbul from Anatolian cities," he says. "And this had to do with class." The people who pulled the strings in the country's mainstream media were the so-called White Turks who lived in Istanbul's elite neighbourhoods. People coming outside their social circles were not welcomed to the world of the media.

"I had a secular lifestyle and yet I worked for the Islamic media," Ünlü says. "At the time the secular elite acted as if they owned the state apparatus. They excluded Islamists and the pious from their publications." In the aftermath of the post-modern coup Ünlü was prosecuted by the infamous State Security Courts where he was accused of publishing documents that featured sensitive information which compromised national security. "At the time the mainstream media was hard at work on producing articles that associated conservatives with terrorism," he says. "Hürriyet, Sabah, Milliyet, Yeni Yüzyıl and Radikal newspapers led the effort. Mainstream

media argued that illegal things were going on among Turkey's Islamists."

At the time Yeni Şafak's columnists included Islamist intellectuals like Nabi Avcı who is now the country's minister of education, as well as liberal-figures like Ali Bayramoğlu, Mehmet Barlas and Cengiz Çandar who found themselves under pressure when they reacted to the military intervention. An aide of an influential general was accused of calling the editor of Sabah newspaper and conveying a threatening message to the paper's liberal columnist Mehmet Altan, who is a professor at

He believes that the country's conservative media is repeating some of the mistakes the mainstream media made in the 1990s

Istanbul University: "I'll make him sit on a bayonet and then I will take him on a tour from one of our borders all the way to the other." The same aide was accused of forcing editors in the mainstream media into firing their dissenting voices. And the country's tense atmosphere reached a new level in 2001 when the Istanbul police raided the offices of Yeni Şafak.

According to Ünlü the real victims of the post-modern coup were headscarved women. "I witnessed how they were pressured from all directions," he says. This is a point shared by Esra Arsan, associate professor of media studies at Bilgi University, who witnessed how headscarved students were expelled from universities. "As members of a liberal university we always defended the rights of our headscarved students," she says. "Bilgi University published Medyakronik, a website that ran critical articles about the mainstream media. As journalism scholars at Bilgi we were critical of the →

→ pressures Islamist media had faced at the time. Then one day Hürriyet newspaper published a front page story with a picture that depicted a lecturer from our university alongside headscarved students who were listening to him in a classroom." At the time Bilgi university allowed headscarved students but shortly after Hürriyet published this picture, which was dutifully enlarged to make the students more visible, the university administration abruptly closed the Medyakronik website before being forced to tighten control over its headscarved students.

Arsan, who is a Reuters Foundation Journalism Fellow at Oxford University, is very critical of the current state of Turkey's media. She says the Islamic media and its secularist opponents share a distaste for the rights of socialists and Kurds and warns that the content of some hardline Islamist papers amounts to hate speech. She also criticises the current government for not giving representatives of the socialist press accreditation for official press briefings. She says the practice reminds her of 1990s when Islamists shared the same fate. She says it is sad to see Islamists being silent about this.

When I asked her about whether Islamic journalists are doing a good job in defending freedom of expression today, Arsan says only a small number of pious journalists share the principle of 'do unto others as you would have them do unto you'. She warns against an atmosphere of revenge and draws parallels with the injustices caused by militarist journalists during 1990s. Although she disagrees with their views, Arsan is skeptical of a legal campaign against old media barons, a view shared by many of her colleagues in the Turkish press.

I ask her about whether the media is more colourful today. "Yes," she says, "in terms of printing techniques it is more colourful". But she finds the content of papers extremely polarizing with most of their columnists focusing on the same narrow issues. She insists on focusing on the problems of the present and says the public should demand more from the mainstream media. "Readers should lead the effort in demanding a more liberal press. They should be the ones demanding the release of imprisoned journalists. Otherwise things will stay the same in Turkey's media," she says.

The Islamic papers are covering the current pressure on the media barons with obvious pleasure. Hardly a day goes by without them publishing an op-ed or a feature that invites the state prosecutors to go after old media barons. And the problem lies exactly there: their triumphant tone echoes that of the old mainstream papers. It seems that Islamist publications are now calling the shots in Turkey's media. The February 28 investigation will show whether the Islamic media will treat its ideological opponents in the same unfair and aggressive way it had accused them of behaving towards itself. X

© Kaya Genc
www.indexforcensorship.org

Kaya Genç is a novelist and essayist based in Istanbul. He tweets at @kayagenc and blogs at www.kayagenc.net

Telling difficult stories

42(4): 31/35 | DOI: 10.1177/0306422013513695

2014 is the tenth anniversary of a British theatre's controversial decision to cancel performances of the play Behzti because of safety concerns after a Sikh protest. Playwright Gurpreet Kaur Bhatti was forced into hiding at the time. **Rachael Jolley** talks to her about censorship, her plays, religious sensitivity and her love for The Archers

GURPREET KAUR BHATTI is about to return to the Birmingham Repertory Theatre, where Behzti (Dishonour) was briefly staged in 2004, with a new play, Khandan (Family). She also writes for the long-running radio soap opera The Archers.

Rachael Jolley: How do you think the arts and culture and freedom of expression have changed in the past 10 years?

Gurpreet Kaur Bhatti: One of the biggest changes is social media, if not the biggest change. So we have a whole other level of expression and participation in debate that didn't exist when Behzti was around.

RJ: How do you think that social media would have affected the production of Behzti in 2004?

GB: You would have had more demonstrators; you'd have had more activity and more discussion on both sides. However, how informed that debate would have been I don't know because I do think that the Twittersphere can reduce things to quite a banal level. The issues are the same and, if anything, they may have got harder because of the economic climate. In some ways our culture has become more fear-ridden. The reasons not to do something are often what people talk about before they even think about what their feelings or even instincts are towards a piece of work.

RJ: Do you think that sort of approach is being shaped by financially difficult times?

GB: In the arts, the notion of the right to fail generally is diminishing, but the issue of offence is a continual struggle and debate and it depends on the person leading the [cultural] institution. The climate is quite difficult for people to act from their hearts and to take risks, which can't be good for artists, for institutions, for people – because provocation and debate are really important.

RJ: How are you feeling about going back to Birmingham?

GB: I actually go back every month because I write for The Archers. But I'm really excited. The Rep has a new artistic director. And I'm looking forward to it. →

ABOVE: A man exits Birmingham Repertory Theatre after the cancellation of Gurpreet Kaur Bhatti's play Behzti in 2004

→ **RJ:** You don't have those memories from 10 years ago sort of crowding in…

GB: You know what, it happened. Life happens. And I have nothing to feel ashamed about or bad about. The theatre pulled my play, which I'm very sad about, but it happened. That play has lived on and that's something that I've spoken about at length, in other ways. It's been studied at universities. It's been performed in Italy, France and Belgium. It's more than me. For me it's a play that I wrote and afterwards I went and did lots of other things. I have written extensively for stage, screen and radio over the past 10 years. So the thing of Behzti is bigger than me and my presence in a city. I don't know how Birmingham will feel. I don't know how certain sections of different communities will feel.

RJ: I suppose the obvious question is: could you see Behzti going on today and would there be a different reaction to it? Has the community moved on?

GB: We've got to be really careful about talking about "the community" because it's not a homogenous lump. Lots of people in the Sikh community were very supportive of me and of the play. I think the sections of the community who weren't …we'd have to see. Are we in a kind of climate where people feel more separatist, feel the need to kind of define themselves more?

I'm sure there will be some people who find it difficult or outrageous but I've just got to get on with what I'm doing and my life and my work and follow that path. I don't think anything has changed in the world to make people stop believing what they believed 10 years ago. Maybe people have mellowed. I don't know.

RJ: Do you feel that the negative reaction came from a sense that part of the Sikh community was not feeling confident of how a wider British identity embraced them or that sense of insecurity?

GB: We've been through so much in this country, so much racism. We've worked so hard. Why the need to kind of, you know, wash dirty linen in public? But for me that's just such a reductive sort of argument. We have stories that we should be able to tell, regardless of who we are. And coming back to religion, as I've said many times before, it was the stuff to do with the faith that people found difficult. I can see that point of view, I understand from a sort of human point of view, but is your faith so weak that it can't bear me and my tiny play?

RJ: Some people have argued that we've moved into a time when people are unwilling to accept a discussion that they think is offensive, particularly if it's about religion. Do you think we have become more sensitive over time to those kinds of discussions?

GB: I think that there is huge over-sensitivity alongside fear and it's not a great combination. Fear and over-sensitivity are deadly to

debate, to progress. I think in order to have a robust conversation about anything we must embark on that conversation with a strong sense of self and robustness and that is sometimes difficult to achieve.

Religions have a lot. They have money. They have buildings. They have structure. They have hierarchy. They have followers. They have literature. An artist is normally one person on his or her own who is doing his or her thing. I don't believe in being a hooligan and just going out and attacking anybody or any institution just for the hell of it but I do think that they have quite a lot of power.

RJ: Do you think there needs to be any sort of sense of a right to reply in theatre as there is in a newspaper?

GB: Again, in social media now you kind of have it. Literally when a show opens at 7.30 people can start tweeting at 7.31. People don't have to buy tickets. We live in a democracy. People are free to demonstrate, free to say they hate something. There are myriads of ways in which people can respond to things they don't like, through social media, through activism, protest. I think that's absolutely as it should be.

RJ: In your view what is the relationship between religious freedom and the right to critique different religions? Do you think that people should be accepting of both?

GB: I think we should be able to do that, but we also need to talk to each other honestly about the things that we don't understand. So if one's critique is based on ignorance then get informed and have a more informed debate. It's about asking ourselves as people, if we want to work in the arts, where there is connection with others.

RJ: So do you think we have a responsibility to be informed before we begin a discussion? →

ABOVE: London's West End theatre district. In the UK, "the issue of offence is a continual struggle and debate", affecting artistic expression and the cultural institutions that support it

→ **GB:** No. It helps, but we are free to say and do what we want within the law. I think there is a lot of Islamaphobia and there is a lot of stuff being talked about Islam that is really uninformed.

You could say the same thing about people on benefits in this country, who are perceived by many, many people as a homogeneous kind of lump. From people who I think should know better. Now they are free to say what they want but if they want to contribute to a serious debate about serious issues then go and get informed.

RJ: We have more media, we have more TV stations, we have more access to social media and more of an ability to find out things from people across the world than we've ever had before.

GB: There's not necessarily a multiplicity of views, of experiences. We think we've got more. Quantitatively we've got more. Qualitatively have we got more? I don't know.

RJ: Do you think there are subjects and areas that playwrights or TV and radio writers won't touch?

GB: I think writers will always write stuff. Whether it gets made is a different thing and that comes down to commissioners and producers and, again, comes down to institutions willing to take risks. I don't think there is an issue that I personally would think "oh god, I couldn't go there". I might not write a play about fishing because I'm not interested in it. When I talk to young writers I always say, you have to be brave, you have to be brave to do this and not be sensationalist for the sake of it.

RJ: Do you think that new media and social media give you more opportunities in some ways?

GB: The fact that people can make a video and put it on YouTube is amazing. There

Credit: © LondonPhotos/Alamy

are brilliant elements of it in terms of communication, in terms of freedom of expression, in terms of people being creative and taking ownership of their thoughts.

RJ: I just want to go back to one thing about whether you felt Behzti could be put on today…

GB: I think it could be. I mean if somebody wanted to do it I'd be very open to talking to them.

RJ: And have you had any approaches to put it on recently?

GB: Not in this country.

RJ: But do you think if it came out, it would be a different version?

GB: Oh no, I'd keep it the same play. The story of that play is that I wrote it really quickly and suddenly it was on. So it was a little bit rough around the edges. But I wouldn't change anything central to it. If people were offended then they would be offended now. So I would just kind of tidy it up in a playwriting sense. I hope that people would see it as a piece of theatre, which is what I always wanted.

RJ: So it could be produced without that sort of anger?

GB: I hope it could be made without that sort of sensationalism around it. It would be up to a director or producer who liked the play and wanted to do it for its theatrical worth rather than anything else.

RJ: So it's not something that, for instance, say, the Birmingham Rep has come back and said: "It's been 10 years, we'd love to put it on?"

GB: They haven't, no. But they are doing my new one so that's good. They're enabling me to express myself.

RJ: So how does The Archers fit in with the playwriting? Do you have different days for different things?

GB: When you do The Archers you do a week of episodes and so that's what I'm doing at the moment. But I only do that four or five months of the year. So I have lots of time for doing my plays. It involves quite a lot of juggling but it's all right.

RJ: It does tackle issues. All soaps do, I suppose, but it has something very Middle England about it.

GB: It's an institution. People find it hilarious that I write for it and that I write the sort of plays that I write. But for me it's two aspects of myself and I really enjoy it. I think the show has great integrity and truth. It's a lovely, lovely job. ☒

©Rachael Jolley
www.indexoncensorship.org

Rachael Jolley is editor of Index on Censorship

Khandan will run at the Birmingham Rep from 22 May to 7 June 2014

Religion rules

42(4): 36/40 | DOI: 10.1177/0306422013513858

Alexander Verkhovsky studies the new blasphemy act and discusses why freedom of religion and belief continue to cause conflict in post-Soviet Russia

TWO ISSUES PREOCCUPYING post-Soviet society are a wish to oppose outside influences (mainly from the West), and to resist aggressive behaviour in matters of religion. It is not difficult to point out inconsistencies and contradictions in these approaches, but more germane is the fact that both have survived, if in modified form, to the present day. When the possibility of further restrictions on freedom of conscience are being discussed, a key topic is invariably the need to protect society from the "expansionism" of new religious movements and radical Islam.

The arrests of members of the Pussy Riot punk band after their performance outside Moscow's Cathedral of Christ the Saviour proved a powerful catalyst for both these concerns. The protest was seen as a frontal attack on "tradition" by "pro-Western forces" (the actual point Pussy Riot wanted to make was neither here nor there), and as an attack on the religious sensibilities of the "Orthodox majority". The reaction was accordingly heavy-handed, including not only imprisonment of two members of the group, but also the passing of a law →

ABOVE: Cathedral of Christ the Saviour in Moscow, where the Pussy Riot performance took place

↑ criminalising the "offending of believers' religious sensibilities", often referred to as the "blasphemy" law.

The legislative proposal was introduced in September 2012 and became law in August 2013 but has not yet been enforced anywhere. There may be at least two reasons for this. First, many laws that are aimed at NGOs, protesters or what is seen as the "opposition" have either been applied much less rigorously than expected or not at all. The authorities have chosen not to resort to wholesale repression, preferring intimidation. Second, the Russian state and its political elite are still very secular and feel uncomfortable about what is widely regarded as a law against blasphemy.

Article 282 of the criminal code in incidents that the law enforcement agencies, victims or others might reasonably have been expected to regard as mere offences against religious sensibilities. In a few cases, charges have been brought and, in fewer still, these charges have led to convictions. From interviews with law enforcement officers and representatives of various religious organisations, it is evident that numerous individuals and organisations that feel they have been offended on religious grounds appeal to the police and prosecutor's office to institute criminal proceedings under Article 282. These requests are almost invariably turned down, and this is not a matter of officials taking sides: they are simply reluctant to institute proceedings on a shaky legal basis, except when that is in their own self-interest. They will do so if there is pressure on them from above, or if they face a pressing need to meet some target.

The addition of this new article to the criminal code, if it is not repealed, will lead sooner or later to its being enforced, and the main source of litigation will be complaints from numerous indignant parties. Demands for charges to be brought rained down upon the prosecutor's office and police even before the amendments became law. It is important to recognise that the problem is not only repressive intentions on the part of the authorities, but also the repressive instincts of Russian citizens. Representatives of a wide range of community interest groups (though, thankfully, by no means all), including a number of minorities, constantly demand that criminal prosecution be the main way to influence those who cause them offence.

If the system does start enforcing this law, freedom of conscience will come under immense new pressure because of the likelihood of the sheer volume of litigation. Enforcement is likely to be highly selective, because a law of this kind can only be applied selectively. It will be manifestly discriminatory, in accordance with some

It is important to recognise that the problem is not only repressive intentions on the part of the authorities, but also the repressive instincts of Russian citizens

Strictly speaking, this is not a law against blasphemy, unlike, for example, similar legislation in Italy. The offence is not against religious doctrine, the deity, or things considered holy. Desecration of sacred objects is an offence not under the Russian Criminal Code, but under the code of administrative offences, which means it is seen as less serious. Offending religious sensibilities or beliefs is a crime in the penal codes of several European countries, but the European Court of Human Rights (and, following it, the Parliamentary Assembly of the Council of Europe) has consistently confirmed that a distinction needs to be made between offending sensibilities and inciting hatred.

In Russia today there are still attempts to bring charges of incitement to hatred under individuals' personal preferences and depending on the government's latest priorities. Finally, it will be completely chaotic, because complaints will come in from all directions and there is nobody remotely qualified to assess their merits.

We can hope, of course, that the new article may yet be removed from the criminal code, but the chances of that are slim. The fact that it is there in the first place results from a consistent trend towards restricting freedom of expression in matters of religion, justified on the basis of the need to maintain "religious peace". There are two main aspects to this laudable aim, and they enjoy widespread support. The first is safeguarding national security against the preaching of terrorism motivated by religion. The second is to safeguard national security against internal, particularly ethnic, conflicts, which are seen as often being fuelled by religion.

These two security aspects were major reasons for the introduction, in 2002-2007, of the current legislation to counteract "extremism". This legislation is used extensively against violent racist groups, but also against sundry ideological minorities, which by no means espouse violence or pose a serious, or indeed any, threat to national security.

Abuse of this legislation is made possible by its imprecise wording, which we also find in respect to the new law to protect religious sensibilities. This inevitably leads to arbitrary application and, specifically, to exploitation for political purposes. There have been numerous instances of this, but let us focus on just three. Among the first major "anti-extremist" trials associated with religion were those targeting contemporary art exhibitions at the Andrey Sakharov Museum, which presaged the Pussy Riot case. Also, in 2011, a journalist was convicted for making rude remarks about believers in general, and the clergy in particular, even though his was not by any means a high profile protest and could not be represented as involving incitement to hatred against any group. Lastly, over several years there has been a serious campaign of criminal prosecution against people who read or distribute the works of a Sufi teacher, the late Said Nursi, even though neither he nor his Russian followers have links to terrorism, or engage in conduct which might constitute a threat to society.

In the case of the Sakharov museum exhibitions, the general public could at least understand more clearly what was going on. Some might consider the exhibition a profound artistic meditation on relations between the church and society; others might see the exhibits as an amusing send-up of the church and/or orthodoxy; some might consider it a send-up in bad taste or even an

A great many of the banned books, websites, videos and material involve religion in one way or another

attack on the church, but within acceptable limits of freedom of expression; others, however, were determined to prove that the exhibition was a criminal incitement to hatred of orthodoxy and Orthodox Christians.

In the case of the persecution of followers of Said Nursi, the general public know nothing about the subject and must either just believe or disbelieve what they are told by the security services, believe or disbelieve what is said by Muslim leaders defending those being persecuted, or simply turn and look the other way. Most people choose the last option, including a majority of journalists, which means a majority of citizens, even those who take an interest in social matters, know nothing about these prosecutions.

Our citizens' understanding of the issues around freedom of conscience is fragmentary. Most are far more concerned about conflicts over the balance between the →

→ slow-but-sure process of de-secularisation and the constitutionally guaranteed secular nature of the state. There are controversies over the presence of religion in schools, about the erection of Orthodox churches and mosques (although in the case of mosques the main cause of dissension is racism), and about various symbols of the cosy relationship between church and state. The real-life problems facing religious groups and, more generally, people expressing an opinion about religion, get forgotten.

These problems are legion. The most acute in recent years have arisen from improper application of anti-extremism legislation, but there are also the more "ordinary" problems, like refusals to release building land for places of worship and systematic campaigns of defamation. In a number of cases, like that of the Jehovah's Witnesses, all these problems come together.

The Federal List of Extremist Materials has, however, excited the public's interest by its scale and, even by Russian standards, sheer absurdity. The list can be found on the website of the Ministry of Justice and itemises materials banned from mass circulation. The ban is imposed by courts at the insistence of local prosecutors, who must satisfy the court that the material contains elements that can be construed as constituting "extremist activity". This is usually incitement to hatred of some sort, impugning the dignity of a group, asserting the superiority or inferiority of a particular religion, and so forth. The whole process is quite remarkably ineffective and does not stand up to scrutiny. Most of the materials the list is seeking to ban cannot be identified from the titles given and, no less problematically, banning them does not in strictly legal terms mean they cannot be re-published, because a new court case would be needed to re-establish the identity of the materials.

A great many of the banned books, websites, videos and material involves religion in one way or another. Many are jihadist texts openly calling for terrorism or other forms of violence, but many have nothing prejudicial in them: perhaps at most a claim of the superiority of one set of beliefs over others, to which texts of Jehovah's Witnesses are prone. There are works by Muslim authors well known for their contribution to jihadist ideology, but on topics that are of no concern to national security (most commonly, on aspects of Sharia law). Finally, a number of texts have found their way on to the list purely by chance, having been confiscated from some "wrong-thinking" individual. This explains the presence of medieval treatises by the likes of the Persian mystic al Ghazali. In 2013 there was even a ban imposed on one of the most popular translations of the Quran.

The absurdity of such methods of "fighting extremism" has obliged even President Putin, at a recent meeting with *muftis* in Ufa in Bashkortostan, to acknowledge that there are problems with the current approach to banning religious materials. Alas, there is no sign of willingness to review the methods of fighting extremism more generally, or those aspects of them that most blatantly violate freedom of conscience. ☒

Translated by Arch Tait
©Alexander Verkhovsky
www.indexoncensorship.org

Alexander Verkhovsky is head of the SOVA Centre for Information and Analysis. He was co-founder and editor-in-chief of samizdat newspaper Panorama

Turning point

42(4): 41/43 | DOI: 10.1177/0306422013513416

International human rights groups have repeatedly failed to acknowledge the dangers of fundamentalism. **Salil Tripathi** talks to Karima Bennoune, whose book Your Fatwa Does Not Apply Here holds a mirror up to Muslim liberals they cannot ignore

KARIMA BENNOUNE IS an Algerian-American lawyer who teaches international law at the University of California, Davis. She is a brave woman. She writes using her real name, travels to dangerous parts of the world and champions men and women who resist fundamentalists.

Bennoune grew up in Algeria amid a struggle of secularists against Islamic fundamentalism. Her father, Mahfoud Bennoune, was an outspoken secularist, a professor at the University of Algiers who faced death threats in the 1990s. She studied at the University of Michigan's law school, and was a delegate at the NGO forum at the world conference on women in Beijing in 1995. She has been a legal adviser at Amnesty International in London and has published widely in legal journals, newspapers and magazines. She was also an election observer in North Africa following the Arab spring.

Your Fatwa Does Not Apply Here begins with a dramatic account of an Islamist mob harassing Bennoune and her father outside their house in June 1993. In the book, Bennoune talks to more than 300 people in 30 countries, who, she says, are "doing today what my father did back then" to build international support for those confronted with fundamentalism. Salil Tripathi spoke

with her during a recent trip to London to launch her book.

Salil Tripathi The debate about Islam and the West is an old one. Most people argue that the key moment was Salman Rushdie's 1988 novel The Satanic Verses. But you show in your book that it is more complex than that.

Karima Bennoune The fatwa on Salman Rushdie was exceptional because it was so transnational and visible. But there are many Rushdies in many contexts. People have taken the most incredible risks to express themselves, without any support. One story that touches me deeply is of an Algerian journalist in the 1990s. Fundamentalists had declared fatwas against the press. Some editors and journalists faced them down, but they were facing prosecution from the government at the same time. Algeria had become the most dangerous place to be a journalist. The story that stays with me is of Omar Belhouchet, the publisher of el Watan. One day he was coming back to his office after attending an assassinated journalist's funeral. He knew people were looking for him, and yet he went to the funeral. As he was returning, he could see smoke from the Press House, a building where many newspapers were located, which had been hit by a truck bomb. →

ABOVE: Karima Bennoune

→ He found that 18 people had been killed – journalists, workers, neighbours. Nearly 60 were injured. Some of the offices were devastated. Journalists were pulling

In the countries where the niqab is worn it is actually a political shackle that is imposed from above

their colleagues from the rubble. Omar gathered the journalists who were unscathed. It was 3pm. He asked: "Who wants to get the paper out?" And they stayed. They worked in the smoky ruins of the Press House, where their colleagues had been killed in a gruesome way. What they did was ferociously

brave journalism. They did a compendium issue of all the newspapers in one. A copy of that compendium is one of my most precious possessions. I remember one of the articles, by Ghania Oukazi, who asked: "Pen against Kalashnikov – is there a more unequal struggle?" And she wrote: "What is certain is that the pen will not stop."

During my research I encountered this time and again. People just kept writing, refusing to be intimidated. Unfortunately, the Rushdie affair is not an anomaly. It represents a much broader attack on freedom of expression, freedom of thought and freedom of movement.

ST And yet, here in the West, and in India where I was born, some people blamed Rushdie for bringing this upon himself. Many of the left, which should have championed writers against fundamentalists, ended up on the side of the fundamentalists. They characterised the Muslims who disagree with them as stooges of the West, or worse.

KB A left-wing Algerian psychologist told me: "No one from among our old friends tells me: 'We are with you.'" It is disappointing; people feel alone. People are left to take risks all by themselves. Cherifa Kheddar, who came to speak in Europe, remembers being heckled by someone from the left who showed up at her talk and denounced her as a stooge of the state. [Kheddar's brother and sister were tortured and murdered by Algerian fundamentalists in her presence in 1996; her husband was also killed. She now runs a victims' support organisation, Djazairouna.]

What's difficult is to find a space to be heard. While I respect those who have left Islam, like Ayan Hirsi Ali – and she should be able to write as she wants to – there are different Islams and different practices. The liberal Islam of my grandfather is what I am fond of. My book can't be accepted by the right, because it is opposed to them, but it is also critical of the left and the human rights movement. I am trying to find another way of talking about this, drawing from the language of the people on the ground. We have seen that the West knows only two sets of responses. On the right, in some quarters, you see anti-Muslim rhetoric – all Muslims are fundamentalists. This is not only offensive, but also wrong. And then on the left, you have a set of responses that are too politically correct to be considered responses at all. Those are flawed and unhelpful positions. I'm looking for another kind of response.

ST What prompted the book?

KB It began in the 1990s, with my father opposing the armed groups in Algeria, when he was threatened with violence. I was frustrated that outside of Algeria people knew so little about it. Years later, we saw the same misunderstandings – a failure to recognise the dangers of fundamentalism. People on the ground in Pakistan, in Chechnya, were doing courageous work, and what was painful for him was that there was so little understanding of this situation outside. So I tried to retrace my father's steps, met these brave people, gave them the microphone.

Local human rights organisations understood exactly what was going on. But in the 1990s, international groups did not understand the threat the ideology of Islamic fundamentalism poses: it is very dangerous for human rights, for women, for free thinkers, for minorities. And the international human rights movement has failed to understand this for a long time. It has also defined the fundamentalist project as "cultural", so that the things that the fundamentalists impose – such as the niqab – are defended as cultural practices. But in the countries where the niqab is worn it is actually a political shackle that is imposed from above.

ST So that was a turning point?

A: Yes, I was personally deeply upset that human rights groups were failing the victims. Jihadi armed groups were committing mass rapes in Algeria, but major international human rights groups were not producing reports on this. And this went on: the way Amnesty International treated Gita Sahgal, despite her dedicated work; the way Amnesty International USA invited Moazzam Begg [the former British prisoner in Guantanamo Bay] to give a keynote address. Begg was rightly defended when he was tortured, but he ran a radical bookshop. [In 2010, Saghal was suspended from Amnesty International after she complained about the group's links to Begg and the email was leaked.] And then there was the case of the Center for Constitutional Rights (CCR), on whose board I sat, which took on a *pro bono* case to defend Anwar al Awlaki, who had issued death threats to prominent people around the world. He was not a detainee being defended. He was advocating that people should be killed. Why did human rights groups not speak out against that? On Awlaki versus Barack Obama we – the CCR – were on Awlaki's side. At that time, seeing Gita's courage in taking on Amnesty, I realised I too had to speak out. ⌧

© Salil Tripathi
www.indexoncensorship.org

Salil Tripathi is a London-based writer and frequent contributor to Index. He co-chairs English PEN's Writers at Risk Committee and is the author of Offence: The Hindu Case (Seagull Books)

Stealth creationists

42(4): 44/46 | DOI: 10.1177/0306422013513117

Sean Gallagher reports on the struggles over school textbooks in Texas, a large and influential state where small-town conservatives and the religious right are trying to get control of editing content

IF BARBARA CARGILL has her way creationism and intelligent design will soon be taught in Texan public schools. Cargill, the chairman of the Texas State Board of Education (SBOE), has called for the repeal of a law that bars the board from reviewing the content of textbooks.

The board currently only has the power to ensure textbooks meet the curriculum, but Cargill is keen for the board to have the powers to review content, and that would mean the board could make changes based on a personal or ideological bias.

Cargill has been labelled "a stealth creationist" by the Texas Freedom Network, an activist group that "advances a mainstream agenda of religious freedom and individual liberties to counter the religious right".

A Republican, Cargill, is also a former biology teacher, from The Woodlands, a community about 30 miles north of Houston. She was elected to the SBOE in 2004, appointed chair of the board by Governor Rick Perry in 2011, and reappointed in 2013.

The law she wants to overturn is Senate Bill 1 passed by the 74th Texas legislature in 1995. The bill was intended to put to rest the culture wars that still erupt on a near annual basis at the SBOE, which oversees curriculum and teaching materials for the second largest education system in the United States. It also updates subject-based standards.

Cargill wants the board to hark back to the days before restrictions on its powers were imposed, a time when the Mel and Norma Gabler, a husband and wife team, began reviewing textbooks from a conservative Christian viewpoint. The organisation the Gablers founded, Educational Research Analysts, based in Longview in east Texas, was the forerunner of other pressure groups who lobby in this area. What these groups have in common is a distrust of anything that smacks of a liberal agenda that might upset their religious beliefs.

Still active today, Educational Research Analysts publishes guidelines advising that health books that make references to "married couples" or "married people" are unambiguous attempts to promote homosexuality. History textbooks, the group maintains, should promote the role of religion in the development of the United States and point out that the Supreme Court gained more power through the "neglect of the original intent of the constitution".

While the Gablers have gone to meet their maker, the tactics they employed have been picked up by the likes of the Texans for Better Science Education and the Discovery

ABOVE: Demonstrators show their support for science education outside the State Board of Education, September 2013, Austin, Texas

Institute, and other conservative groups that promote the theory of intelligent design.

While currently barred from revising textbooks unless they are factually incorrect, the members of the SBOE still do have enormous power to steer the creation of those texts by setting the standards they must aspire to.

In 2010, the SBOE instituted social studies standards that downplayed slavery's role in the Civil War; implied that Senator Joseph McCarthy's communist hunts in the 1950s were justified, and removed the concept

History textbooks, the group maintains, should promote the role of religion in the development of the United States

of "responsibility for the common good", which, according to the Texas Freedom Network, one board member found too communistic.

→ This year's attempt to undermine the presentation of evolution in biology textbooks looks likely to fail because publishers balked at some of the revisions which they considered ideological rather than factual.

Cargill is not the only conservative Christian on the board. The organisation, which is selected in off-year election cycles in a state not known for its voter turnout, attracts large amounts of funding from conservative groups. One former chairman, Don McElroy, an avowed creationist who believes that man and dinosaurs coexisted, told the Washington Times that evolution was "hooey". Cargill herself has lamented that there are only "six true conservative Christians on the board."

Texan and American children need to be able to explore the broadest possible education, free from superstition and based in fact

But the ideological tug of war obscures the real issue with the Texas SBOE — the tyranny of the small. Of the 10 Republicans on the board, only three live in cities that have populations over 500,000. The rest live in towns that range from 16,000 to 200,000 inhabitants. On the Democratic side, only one board member lives in an area with fewer than half a million people.

In general, Texas' small towns are overwhelming white, conservative redoubts, afraid of the larger changes in America's culture. While small town residents are likely to be just as intelligent as city dwellers, they are not exposed to the sheer variety of viewpoints offered by living in a large urban centre.

Texan and American children need to be able to explore the broadest possible education, free from superstition and based in fact,

even theoretical fact. They need an education that ensures that the country can compete on a global scale.

Cargill may not get her wish to strike the law that inadequately restrains the SBOE, but the damage her presence on board continues and her conservative, Christian viewpoint which she inflicts on Texan education system will be felt for decades to come. Textbook publishers are still handcuffed by the standards the State Board of Education continues to enact. All this matters because Texas' textbook market is the second largest in the United States and the print run of a Texas edition goes further than the state borders. X

©Sean Gallagher
www.indexoncensorship.org

Sean Gallagher is editor (online and news) at Index on Censorship. He lived in Texas from 2011 to 2012

ABOVE: Devotees of Sao Jorge, known as Ogum in the Afro-Brazilian Umbanda religion, sing during the celebrations of Sao Jorge's day, Rio de Janeiro

Religious intolerance in the land of festivals

42(4): 48/54 | DOI: 10.1177/0306422013512973

Ronaldo Pelli reports on the growing influence of the neo-Pentecostal church in Brazil, which threatens to drive out traditional Brazilian religions of African origin

HISTORICALLY BRAZIL HAS been seen as a land of festivals and great-tolerance, where races live together harmoniously. The country has a image around the world as a place comfortable embracing different ways of life and different faiths. Recently, however, it has been become clear that this image does not reflect the present reality. Perhaps it never did.

Attacks on the temples of religions such as *Candomblé*, *Umbanda*, and others of similarly African origin-by radical members of neo-Pentecostal churches has turned the subject of religious tolerance into a topic of regular debate.

There has never been a dominant church in Brazil; *Candomblé* and *Umbanda* are among the various religions of African origin that remain popular. They are practised →

→ by people in *terreiros,* or sacred spaces, named as such because they used to be outdoors, though most *terreiros* now are in buildings. Even though few people are prepared to admit that they belong to *Candomblé* or *Umbanda* congregations, it is perfectly normal for members of other faiths, especially Catholics, to visit the *terreiros*. People attend to invoke intercessions they may not be able to access through the mainstream churches, for example if they need help in their love lives, or have illnesses they need cured. They also go to *terreiros* for divinations and predictions for the future.

Brazil is nevertheless the largest Catholic nation in the world, and the Catholic church also boasts the largest black population out-

Attacks on religions of African origin reached intolerable levels

side of Africa. So religions of African heritage have had to adapt to the demands and conditions of a Brazilian reality.

In the case of *Candomblé,* its history is bound up with that of Africans trafficked as slaves to the Americas and the religion has been practised since the beginning of Portuguese colonisation. Its rituals are founded upon respecting the faith and dancing and singing. Offerings and animal sacrifices are made to the ancestors, and to the Orixas, the gods represented by the forces of nature.

Officially, the Portuguese never tolerated non-Catholic practices in its colonies. For example, in 1832 a decree was issued obliging slaves to convert to Catholicism. Any individual accused of fetishistic customs was punished and could even face the death penalty. So Africans adopted the saints of the Catholic church and began to worship them under African names. St George became Ogum; St Lazarus became Omulu and Santa Barbara, Yansa.

Umbanda is of more recent origin, and dates from the start of the 20th century. As well as Portuguese influence, there are also indigenous ones.

Historian and professor Washington Dener dos Santos Cunha from the State University of Rio de Janeiro is a specialist in African history. He says that during the 1930s and 40s the *Umbanda* community, which had come to include both *caboclos* (descendents of Indians and whites) and *pretos-velhos* (the descendants of former slaves), tried to develop a discourse with the government about Brazilian identity. "This happened principally over the period of the *Estado Novo* or New State, which existed between 1937 and 1945 and was the name given to the dictatorship government headed by President Getulio Vargas," he says. "It was at a time when Getulio Vargas was seeking to consolidate his policy of a Brazilian racial democracy and create a land in which there were no racial conflicts and where everyone lived in harmony."

To Marcio Alexandre M Gualberto, the author of The Map of Religious Intolerance 2011: the Violation of the Right to Free Worship in Brazil, such persecutions of the principal religions of African origin on the part of neo-Pentecostalists has arisen because of competition for new congregations. "As is commonly said of Brazil, everyone frequents the *terreiro* and everyone there beats a drum. Notwithstanding this, there is a more specific public being fought over. It is noteworthy that neo-Pentecostal churches are establishing themselves in places where there are few Catholic or Protestant ones, but where, invariably, there is a *terreiro* dedicated to Axe, god of energy and the life force. That is where they install themselves and pick a fight to win over the established congregation."

Expulsions and segregation

The growth of so-called neo-Pentecostal sects has mainly occurred in the most impov-

ABOVE: A tiny evangelical Pentecostal church on Ilha do Marajo fluvial island in the Amazon, Para state, northern Brazil

erished corners of the country. The most radical members of the new faithful in the neo-Pentecostal sects have made violent common cause with organised criminals, who already have a high degree of control over the poorest areas, given the absence of a state presence. And that has led to members of Afro-Brazilian faith communities being expelled from the *favelas* of Rio.

The Rio newspaper Extra, one of the most popular in Brazil, in its 7 September 2013 issue, coincidentally the date on which Brazilian independence from Portugal is celebrated, carried a report on the subject.

According to the article, there are now more than 40 documented cases of members of the *Candomblé* and *Umbanda* faiths who, in addition to having been prevented from practising their religions, have been thrown out of their own homes.

"There was no way to survive such a threat. In those places it is simply impossible to be part of *Candomblé*. There are no more *terreiros* and where the religion is still practised, it has to be followed in secrecy," a *filha de santo*, as *Umbanda* devotees are called, explained. She did not wish to disclose her name for fear of reprisals. →

→ She was obliged to leave the Morro do Amor, one of the slums in the so-called Complexo do Lins, in Rio's Zona Norte, to live in the Zona Oueste, which is much further out of the city. Coincidentally or not, the Lins *favela* was allocated one of the Police Pacification Units (PPUs) about a month after publication of the report.

The PPUs are the present government's main device for dealing with public safety. The objective is to install small units of police in lawless areas governed by criminals who use guns to impose their own law.

Even today the state itself participates in racial segregation. The present constitution, dating back to 1988, which guarantees liberty of religious expression, determines that the places where rites and their liturgies are celebrated should be protected by law. Some may be surprised then by the official manner in which the constitution is implemented.

In Maranhao, one of the poorest states in Brazil, the State Public Ministry established an accord with the leader of the local *Umbanda* community, the *pai de santo*, Mauricio dos Santos Mota. The accord restricted the celebration of the cult only to Fridays, between 6pm and 9pm, and without the use of traditional musical instruments. The Spirit of Umbanda Centre of Our Lady of the Candelaria which, as its name suggests, has a Roman Catholic patron saint, also formally agreed to leave the place it had long occupied to move to another, far more remote and worse place.

If the contract was not complied with, Father Mauricio, as he is widely known, would be subject to legal consequences and a police investigation would be set in train. This happened despite a federal law dating back to 1997 that has severe penalties for religious discrimination. A rapid internet search gives us numerous other examples of attacks on the *terreiros*, in all parts of the country. There are no official statistics with which to document the number of violations of the right to freedom of belief, but the Secretariat of the

Policies for the Promotion of Racial Equality from the Presidency of the Republic (Seppir) reports a sharp rise in the number of complaints brought to its attention.

Luiza Bairros, the Minister for Seppir, appears to confirm this. At an event organised to celebrate the National Day to Combat Religious Intolerance on 21 January 2013, she argued that the attacks on religions of African origin had reached intolerable levels. "The worst part is not just that of the considerable number of cases, but the gravity of the cases. They include physical aggression, and threats of destruction of homes and whole communities. It does not only constitute a religious dispute, but also the struggle for civilised values."

Again, this trajectory of religions of African origin in the context of Brazilian history is not reflected in the statistics. In the 2010 census, the practitioners of *Umbanda* and *Candomblé* combined did not add up to even 0.5 per cent of the population. Professor Dener dos Santos Cunha explains that there are multiple reasons for this. Among them is the extremely conciliatory nature of such faiths: it is quite normal for the faithful to frequent other churches as well. When they responded to the census, they would usually describe themselves as either Catholic or Spiritualist in order to avoid preconceptions, or through mere inertia.

The rise of neo-Pentecostal religions

Neo-Pentecostal religions started to undergo a sudden growth in the 1990s, but the tendency dates back still further. For the purposes of comparison, over the past 50 years the Brazilian population grew by 63.2 per cent, while the number of evangelicals expanded by 93.3 per cent.

In 2010, 22.2 per cent of the national population of almost 200 million inhabitants described themselves as evangelicals. In 2000, it had been 15.4 per cent; in 1991, 9 per cent; and in 1980, 6.6 per cent.

The proportion of Catholics has also diminished. They constituted 99.7 per cent of the population in 1872, and being Catholic then was synonymous with being Brazilian. Now, according to the most recent figures available, they number no more than 64.4 per cent of the population.

This increase in the number of neo-Pentecostals is not the fruit of greater religious devotion, but of the appearance of new social values in Brazil, the theologian Orivaldo Pimentel Lopes Junior, professor at the Federal University of Rio Grande do Norte and author of the book *Novas Perspectivas sobre o Protestantismo Brasileiro* (New Perspectives on Brazilian Protestantism) says. He writes, "Economic rationalisation, the legal ordinances of the secular and democratic state, universal education, changes in the agrarian structure, among other elements typical of the modern state, only occur in tandem with the cultural changes conducive to the end of a religious monopoly on the part of Roman Catholicism." He makes clear that economic rationalisation may also carry a high price because it promotes an excess of individualism. "Its political effects are still for the most part felt by the electorate and corporations," he writes.

Hand-in-hand with their growth in strength outside Brazil's Congress goes the participation of the block formed by representatives of these neo-Pentecostal churches inside Brazil's legislative power.

There was an increase of 50 per cent in the number of evangelical Congressmen and women in the period between the last two elections. These politicians indicate through their voting patterns a conservative, if not a reactionary, tendency. The Evangelical Parliamentary Front (FPE), for example, is a non-aligned group established in 2003 to defend the vested interests of followers of these religions. They have 79 parliamentary deputies and senators out of a total 513 federal deputies and 81 senators overall.

The sociologist Ricardo Mariano, professor at the Pontifical Catholic University (PUC) of Rio Grande do Sul and author of *Neopentecostais: sociologia do novo penecostalismo no Brazil* (Neo-Pentecontalists: the Sociology of new Pentecostalism in Brazil) says, "In defence of morality and of good order, the FPE joins forces with deputies linked to groups of conservative Catholics in order to fight, for example, against the Project of the Law number 122/2006, which criminalises homophobia, considering it an attack on religious liberty and freedom of expression. The Front also radically opposes the decriminalisation of the private use of certain drugs, the legalisation of euthanasia and of brothels and the

The growth of neo-Pentecostal sects has mainly occurred in the most impoverished corners of the country

termination of pregnancy before the twelfth week, following the medical opinion of a doctor or psychologist."

It is difficult to make any sweeping generalisation on institutions that differ so completely from one another, but this individualistic character could be marked as among the most radical characteristic of these churches. "He who is not with you is against you," concludes the historian and professor at Rio's Fluminense Federal University, Marcos Alvito, demonstrating how the neo-Pentecostal vision of the world is marked by the concept of a spiritual war, in which the principal opponents in the religious field are deemed demonic. He says, "They are obsessed with combating Afro-Brazilian cults of *Umbanda* and *Candomblé*, described in such derogatory terms as *macumbaria*, fetishism and black magic. This fierce attack is all the harsher within the sub-group of certain churches of a →

→ neo-Pentecostal tendency, among which the most famous is the Universal Church of the Kingdom of God." Alvito adds that the Universal Church (also known by the acronym IURD) has itself also adopted certain magical practices drawn from Afro-Brazilian religions, adapting them to give an inverted and "positive" significance.

IURD provides an interesting instance of the power of the neo-Pentecostal churches. They own churches spread through 96 countries of the world. In Brazil they own the Record Television Network, which has the second largest broadcast audience in the country, in addition to owning newspapers, radio stations, websites and other media outlets. There are even strong signs of a close connection to the Republican Party of Brazil, a political group to which ex-Vice President Jose Alencar, who died in 2011, belonged.

"The polarised vision of the Pentecostal church is not exactly compassionate towards Afro-Brazilian religions, such an important element in our overall Brazilian cultural heritage. In the face of this world vision, the creation of peaceful forms of co-existence between different religions, in accordance with Brazilian law, will daily become a bigger and more important challenge for each of us," Alvito concludes. X

Translated by Amanda Hopkinson
©Ronaldo Pelli
www.indexoncensorship.org

Ronaldo Pelli is a freelance journalist based in Rio de Janeiro. He writes regularly for Revista de História da Biblioteca Nacional

 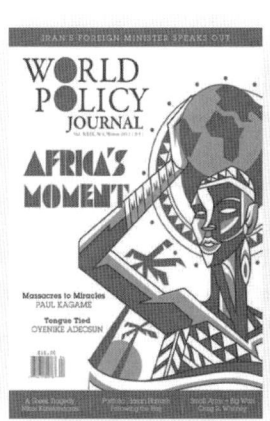 
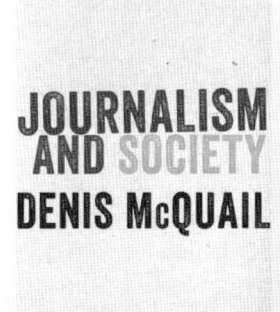  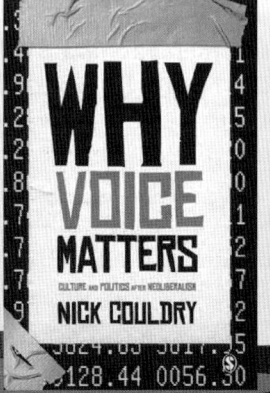  

Laugh out loud

42(4): 56/61 | DOI: 10.1177/0306422013512244

Cartoonist and writer **Martin Rowson** on the need to be allowed to poke fun at religious subjects without fear of retribution or legislation

"BE NOT DECEIVED; God is not mocked." That's obviously true. After all, it's in the Bible, so it must be. And religion is one of those things that is so personal to the individual believer that to mock the object of his or her devotions is certainly the grossest form of personal disrespect. Isn't it?

In the war between freedom of expression and its various enemies, the skirmishes over the right to be critical of religion and the equal – yet opposite – right not to be needlessly offended appear to be the most fraught. Worse, spies exist on both sides. Why, for instance, is it acceptable to abuse someone's religion when those who dole out this abuse often believe that abuse on grounds of race or gender or sexuality is actually a taboo? How can so-called progressive secularists be so unremittingly beastly to largely poor, mostly kind and usually blameless people because they believe in something that makes their life meaningful but which the progressive secularists abhor as delusional? Why should religion (or, more pertinently, some religions) be fair game for criticism when the manifest and obvious shortcomings of the critics can't be? Worst of all, how can it be acceptable to laugh at religion, given its central, and maybe even defining, role in the lives of countless numbers of people throughout human history?

Hence those unending rows continue to erupt with considerable frequency. There's the notorious case of the cartoons of the Prophet Mohammed published in the Danish newspaper Jyllands-Posten in September 2005, which ultimately led to more than a hundred people being killed, though none of them were cartoonists and all of them were Muslims, shot dead on the streets of Muslim countries by Muslim soldiers or policemen after having been incited to protest by Muslim clerics. More recently, in October 2013, the London School of Economics (LSE) Students' Union banned members of the LSE Atheist, Secularist and Humanist Student Society from wearing T-shirts featuring the online comic strip Jesus and Mo at the university's Freshers' Fair following complaints from students. LSE's Legal and Compliance Team and Head of Security told the society that wearing the T-shirts, which depicted the founders of the Christian and Islamic religions, could amount to "harassment" and could be seen as creating an "offensive environment".

Indeed, when it comes to the rows revolving around religion and humour, cartoons seem to be the most frequent *casus belli*. I know this from personal experience, and also know why people are so affronted by them. As it happens, that's got less to do with religion than with the medium: cartoons are, in effect, a very primitive kind of

sympathetic magic, calculated to harm through mockery, but they also have far greater powers to offend thanks to the direct and mostly unmediated way that they're consumed. (Or do I mean "read"? "Seen?" Interestingly, there doesn't seem to be a precise English word for how an audience interacts with cartoons, almost as if this process involves an unsayable, nearly mystical mystery). That said, over the years I seem to have succeeded in deeply offending Catholics, Protestants, Muslims, Jews, Hindus and, for that matter, atheists, as well as Republicans, Democrats, Zionists, Islamists, Serbs, the fat, the mentally ill and, thanks to a recent cartoon depicting a jovial if sinister loan shark, shark lovers (I'm guilty, it seems, of the crassest kind of anthropomorphism, unjustly defaming these harassed predators of the deep).

That last example might seem risible, though not, perhaps, if you are rightly affronted by the fact that 10 million sharks were either killed or mutilated for their dorsal fins last year. Still, should that mean that sharks should be protected through the sanctions of the criminal law from hate speech, including drawings? And should that also include jokes? And, if not, why should religions be treated any differently from sharks?

The statement "God is not mocked" doesn't answer that question. Stripped of the cultural and historical heft it enjoys as the written part of the machinery of control that Christianity exercised over vast swathes of humanity for around a millennium and half, it's just a hope, a wish. Taken from Chapter Six, Verse Seven of St Paul's Epistle to the Galatians, the statement's wider context was Paul's programme of severing Christianity from its roots in Judaism by downgrading the significance of circumcision. Many commentators have accounted to Paul the mutation of Jesus's insurrectionist sect into the kind of totalitarian religion Christianity became, and which it remains in many of its various forms (though by no

means in all of them). It shares its prescriptive and totalitarian nature with branches of Islam, with which it also shares its origins in Judaism, the religion that, in its monotheistic guise, possibly evolved out of Persian Zoroastrianism.

The verse continues: "for whatsoever a man soweth, that shall he also reap," which doesn't get us much further. However, the Old Testament, usually considered to be more robust in these matters, helpfully states in Isaiah 28:22: "Now therefore, do not be mockers, lest your bonds be made strong; for I have heard from the Lord God of hosts, a destruction determined upon the whole earth." That, you have to admit, is more like it. To paraphrase very loosely, it says, "if you take the piss, the creator of the universe is gonna get ya!" But at its heart it still says little more than "Don't laugh at me, or you'll get it!" That's an understandable human response, so we need to delve a lot deeper

Cartoons are, in effect, a very primitive kind of sympathetic magic

into the nature of ourselves than any religious texts will take us.

To begin with, when I asserted a few paragraphs ago that religion has defined people throughout human history, I should have qualified that statement by affirming that history – which is usually defined as the written record of human events – is very young compared to humans' time as a species on the planet. Our species of hominid has been around, it's reckoned, for roughly 200,000 years. "Civilisation" – that is, settled human communities based around agriculture – and "history" – the record that permits us to know more or less what happened – have existed for not much longer than what's often called "Biblical time", that is, the period that spans not much →

⑦ **God is not Mocked!!!**

⑧ WELL IF THAT'S YOUR ATTITUDE MAYBE I JUST WON'T BOTHER BEING CREATED AFTER ALL!

No no no no no no no!!! You can't pull out at this stage!

WANNA BET

But you must be created! Sob!! Pleeeeeeeeeeeeeease!!!

SHAN'T!

⑨ OH ALL RIGHT THEN! HOW ABOUT THIS? I WON'T MOCK YOU IF YOU DON'T MOCK ME! SO, NO TAKING THE PISS WITH ANY OF THAT MISERY, SIN OR DEATH BOLLOCKS! DEAL?

You're on!

→ longer than the 6,000 years that the 17th Century Irish Archbishop James Ussher calculated was the age of the Earth. In other words, what we think of as human history covers about three to four per cent of actual human history. There is, furthermore, no evidence whatsoever that the kind of totalitarian monotheistic religions that appear to be least able to tolerate jokes about themselves have been around for more than around 2,500 years. Meanwhile, extrapolations from the archeological record remain mostly guesswork: pre-Neolithic artwork

Laughter and mockery are among the instinctive tools we use to help us navigate through life

may have religious significance and it may not; it might even be argued that the exaggerated and stylised animals painted in the Chauvet caves in southern France 32,000 years ago (that is, at least 24,000 years before agriculture) are more like cartoons or caricatures than anything else, with equal amounts of spiritual or transcendental content or significance. This, though, could just be my special pleading.

That said, clever geneticists have traced humans' ability to laugh back through the gene sequences five million years to our hominid distant ancestors. Which makes laughter a thousand times older than what we chiefly understand as organised religion. Moreover, there's no reason whatsoever to assume that homo sapiens have altered much physiologically during our existence; or that we're no longer good at the things we do well, like sex and jumping and laughter and empathy; or that what progress we've made has been limited to the areas that we were previously bad at, like maths or flying or keeping a straight face.

More than that, over a century and a half of ethnographic studies of still-existing pre-agricultural peoples have all come to the same conclusion: that hunter-gatherer groups of humans, living as our species has done for 96 per cent of its time on Earth, are fiercely pro-actively egalitarian and cooperative, using many different strategies to prevent the development of hierarchies and the emergence of alpha males. These strategies include murder, ostracism and, naturally, mockery. In his 2001 book Hierarchy in the Forest, the primatologist and anthropologist Christopher Boehm cites many examples of mockery being used as a social control. For example, among the Kung people of the Kalihari, a particularly good hunter will try to exert autonomy over the rest of the group by showing off the antelope he's just killed; the rest of the group respond with sarcastic comments along the lines of "Call that an antelope? Wanker!" In another example, the shaman of an Amazonian tribe tried vainly to bend the rest of the group to his will by threatening them with the terrible things the gods will do to them if they don't obey him; sadly for him, everyone else ended up laughing at him, and his gods.

But we don't need anthropologists to point out human truths we all recognise, because laughter and mockery are among the instinctive tools we use to help us navigate through life and the experience of living with other people. So we all have a basic understanding about how to use humour to attract people and to repel, to forge bonds and break them, and even if we're not that funny ourselves, we understand its potency. That's why lonely hearts ads seek out potential sexual partners with a GSOH (good sense of humour); why stadia are filled with comedians telling jokes; and why a farting raspberry blown on the belly of a child under the age of one anywhere on Earth will automatically make them dissolve in laughter.

It's also why we laugh at shit and sex and death – to make the inevitable realities of life both bearable and controllable. We also laugh at power and otherness, for identical reasons. And all that laughter does things to us: it releases endorphins that make us happy, and happy to be with other people who also make us laugh. However much life might seem a vale of tears, getting people to laugh has never been a problem. The real trick is to get them to stop.

As I've suggested, the priests emerged comparatively recently, around the same time as the kings. What both demanded of other people was something much harder and less natural than laughter: they demanded respect and obedience. The measure of how hard it was for people to respond the way the priests and kings demanded is evidenced by the extraordinarily disproportionate punishments meted out for defiance to the new "laws" of treason and blasphemy. In the case of religion, the cruelty was extended from torturing the living to promising the torture and cruelty would continue even after death. This cruelty was punishment for disobedience or refusal to believe preposterous things – about imaginary creatures or the superiority of kings – which are, in all other circumstances, wholly laughable.

I think there are several key elements we can glimpse in the mists of pre-history that have helped define the way we are now, and which turn things on their head. Maybe it's not so much that God is not mocked, but that God has been created as something so unimaginably vast and terrifying simply to stop the mockery and terrorise the mockers into silence and obedience; that things are deemed sacred – in the same way as other things are deemed to be taboo – because in all other circumstances they'd be ridiculous.

We still live with this legacy. The terrible earnestness and seriousness of our leaders cows us into allowing them to commit any number of appalling crimes, including murder; the po-facedness of the priests not only stops us having fun, but prevents us from having a laugh at preposterous nonsense like virgin births and hidden imams and being alive after we're dead and all the rest of it. Permitting even the slightest giggle allows for the possibility of it all melting into air. When you consider that religious identity is such a potent political force, operated by those with power and without it, it's no wonder that God is not mocked, even if it's infinitely more human to make sure he, she, it or they are. After all, everything else is mocked. ☒

©Martin Rowson
www.indexoncensorship.org

Martin Rowson's cartoons appear regularly in the Guardian and Index on Censorship. His books include The Dog Allusion (Vintage), Giving Offence (Seagull) and Fuck: the Human Odyssey (Random House)

Not waving, not listening

42(4): 62/65 | DOI: 10.1177/0306422013513386

A controversy over when to fly the Union Jack above Belfast city hall has culminated in a small but significant crackdown on civil liberties in Northern Ireland, says **Padraig Reidy**

NORTHERN IRELAND SHOULD really have gone away by now. We'd all agreed, surely. There was a peace process and then there was an assembly and everyone gets along now. Well, not quite gets along, but they've learned to live with each other.

That's what the rest of the world told itself.

One spring morning earlier this year, I came across a procession in London's Whitehall. A small group, overwhelmingly made up of middle-aged white men, was marching towards the Houses of Parliament, waving Union Jacks. The march had been called by an offshoot of the English Defence League, the South East Alliance, and was the first incursion of Belfast's ongoing "flags" (or "flegs" for those who took it less seriously) controversy into the British capital.

The flags issue blew up in Belfast in December 2012. The city council was set to vote on the apparently innocuous question of whether to fly the Union flag on just 18 specified days per year – in line with most town halls in the UK – rather than every day.

Councillors cannot have imagined what would happen next. As they voted, hundreds of Protestants gathered outside to protest. A mob attempted to storm the city hall. In the following days, a video of a middle-aged woman screaming "No surrender!" through a broken window went viral around the world. The protests went on throughout the winter. The summer saw loyalist clashes with police – not unusual, but certainly given extra vim by the flags controversy. As I write, there are still spill-over protests against the perceived threat to "PUL" (Protestant, Unionist, Loyalist) culture.

Why did this happen?

The correctly held opinion is that the flag movement blew up because of a loyalist working class competing for increasingly squeezed resources in austere times. The dismissive opinion is that these people are always fighting about something, and this is just the latest thing. The clever opinion is that the loyalist paramilitary groups that traditionally held sway in Belfast's Protestant neighbourhoods have lost their grip, and a new wave of young people, who don't remember the horror of the long, bloody conflict, have stepped up, looking for their own bit of excitement.

ABOVE: Protesters outside Belfast City Hall, Northern Ireland, February 2013

Certainly, the city councillors who voted on what seemed a minor piece of housekeeping cannot have envisaged this.

Which is not to say that this is an entirely organic movement. Students of Northern Irish politics will recognise some of the key figures among the "fleggers". At their head is Willie Frazer.

Frazer is a middle-aged, bespectacled Armagh man who, it must be said, looks an unlikely leader of a street movement. In the late 1990s, he was the founder of the Families Acting for Innocent Relatives (FAIR) campaign, which claimed to stand for victims of the Provisional IRA in south Armagh.

Frazer's own father, an Ulster Defence Regiment officer, was killed by the IRA. Frazer was also the man behind the Love Ulster group, which was supposedly set up to promote PUL culture. That movement's highlight came in 2006 when an attempted loyalist march through Dublin, the capital of the Republic of Ireland, sparked a riot.

Alongside Frazer was a young born-again Christian called Jamie Bryson. Bryson, from the picturesque town of Donaghadee, County Down, came to prominence in September 2012 with the publication of the first in a trilogy of ebooks called 50 Shades of God, marketed as an appeal to get young →

→ people interested in Christianity. The Amazon blurb for the book makes rather grand claims:

"Hailed by some as a God inspired 'turn it all upside down' blueprint and dismissed by others as a book to be kept out of the public domain.

"One church said 'this book should be banned, it is too radical and has the potential to inspire too many minds for radical change.' Read for yourself and make your own mind up. How dangerous can one man's opinion really be?"

But aside from the Bible-bashing, Bryson had form in loyalist politics. He had been prominent in the North Down Somme Society (the Battle of the Somme is prominent in loyalist mythology), and at one point co-founded a political party with some fellow "community workers".

Authorities have been all too willing to cast free expression aside when those who question the peace process settlement are involved

According to Northern Irish political website Slugger O'Toole, other major players included Mark Gordon, a reformed glue-sniffer who is now a Protestant pastor, and Jonny Harvey, a former RAF pilot who was a member of a group called Ulster Protestant Voice before joining the Progressive Unionist Party a year ago.

This strange crew managed to prolong the crisis over the course of 2013. At the beginning of the protests, it was clear the authorities did not have a handle on what was happening. The flag protests continued throughout December 2012, and were blamed for a slump in Belfast city centre business in the run-up to Christmas, as shoppers stayed away. Water cannons were deployed

against the protesters as the police struggled to douse the flames of what appeared to be spontaneous anger against the police, republicans, the Stormont government – and, most of all, the non-sectarian Alliance party.

The Alliance delegation on the city council had been responsible for the suggestion that the flag be flown on 18 specific days (nationalists had wanted the UK flag removed from the city hall entirely, Unionists had wanted it to stay in place all year round). This was perceived by the flag protesters as a terrible betrayal, in spite of the fact that Alliance is not an avowed Unionist party.

Alliance party offices were attacked and attempts were made to set it on fire, while the party's one MP, Naomi Long, received death threats.

While the attacks on Alliance eventually abated, the movement went on. In April, Frazer set up the Protestant Coalition, a pressure-group-cum-political-party, along with Jim Dowson, an anti-abortion activist and former British National Party (BNP) fundraiser. Apart from flags, the group's main activity seems to be posting a variety of statements on Facebook, desperately garnering likes and shares with pictures of the royal family and cute dogs – really – and occasionally getting blocked from the social network website. The multiple deletions and reinstatements have led Protestant Coalition leaders to claim that Facebook, which has its European headquarters in Dublin, is riddled with republicans who are prejudiced against Protestant loyalists.

Watching the various contortions, cock-ups and conspiracies embarked upon by the leaders of the flag protests can be darkly amusing. In March, Gordon announced that Bryson, who was in police custody, was about to embark on a hunger strike. Hours later Bryson asked police to order an Indian takeaway meal for him. In September, Willie Frazer turned up at court dressed as Islamist preacher Abu Hamza, in protest at being prosecuted under a law

he said had been created to counter jihadist terror. Bryson, for reasons unclear, dressed as singer Jon Bon Jovi. Northern Ireland's budding internet satirists, among them the people behind "Loyalists Against Democracy", have been having the time of their lives with the protesters.

But while it is easy to laugh at Frazer and friends, what is happening to them is troubling. The leaders of the protests have been repeatedly arrested and jailed throughout the year. Frazer's protest against charges of "encouraging offences with an address" was equal parts ridiculous and well-founded. As Northern Irish commentator Newton Emerson tweeted: "As usual, the real problem with Willie Frazer is that he has a point."

Bryson and Frazer have been subjected to some bizarre restrictions: Bryson at one point was barred from talking about the flags controversy in public. The two men are not allowed to speak on the phone.

The progress made in Northern Ireland since the Good Friday agreement of 1998 has been remarkable. But the process does not brook dissent from those outside the mainstream who have not signed up. The power-sharing executive means that there is essentially no official political opposition, as parties that previously represented extremes (the Democratic Unionist Party and Sinn Féin) now govern together.

From Bryson and Frazer to Suzanne Breen, the journalist who was hounded by the Northern Ireland police while reporting on the actions of dissident republicans, Northern Ireland's authorities have been all too willing to cast free expression aside where those who question the peace process settlement are involved.

The flags protesters are not ideal poster boys for free expression, but then there is rarely such a thing. Northern Ireland will have to find a way to include even dissenters in the new settlement, or these anguished, incoherent and occasionally violent cries will become louder and more frequent. ☒

©Padraig Reidy
www.indexoncensorship.org

Padraig Reidy is senior writer at Index on Censorship

Online mission

42(4): 66/68 | DOI: 10.1177/0306422013513407

Mormons are using the web to talk to the world about their religion.
Brian Pellot chats to the church online to see how it is using the web
to connect with new converts

"WELCOME TO MORMON.ORG chat. A missionary will be with you shortly. Please continue to hold for the next available missionary."

What sounds like a customer service dead end is actually the automated start of a session on missionary chat, from the Church of Jesus Christ of Latter-day Saints.

Logging in to missionary chat one Sunday afternoon this autumn to see how the church's teens and twentysomethings are using digital technologies to reach new audiences, I found missionaries at chat centres in Provo and Salt Lake City, Utah, in the United States, greeted me with delight. Beyond Utah and the continental US, online missionaries cover multiple time zones, for instance, in Hawaii, in the United Kingdom and in New Zealand.

Elder David F. Evans, executive director of the church's missionary department, recently discussed how new technologies and social media are changing the missionary's traditional role.

"Social media and technology is a wonderful development for missionary work," he said, noting that many young missionaries and church leaders are now using Facebook and Twitter to preach the gospel. The Mormon.org Facebook page has 3.3 million likes and @LDSChurch has more than 78,000 fol-

lowers on Twitter. That's impressive considering there are only about 15 million Mormons worldwide.

Evans expects that more missionaries will start using tablets, smartphones and new social media platforms to enhance their work in the coming year. "We anticipate that this technology and the use of digital devices will begin to be broadly available throughout all of the world where it's safe to do so and where we can legally do so," he said.

That legal caveat is a crucial one. At last count more than 80,000 Mormon missionaries were serving in more than 150 countries. But in many predominantly Muslim states and countries such as China, Cuba and North Korea, Mormons are legally barred from preaching the gospel or converting new members to the church.

Mormon.org launched in 2001 to provide an official portal for news and information about the church. In 2008 the chat function was added, providing missionaries a new way to answer basic questions about their beliefs. Hundreds of baptisms have resulted from conversations that began on Missionary Chat in the past five years, and up 5,000 strangers sign in each month.

Mormon officials and missionaries say they respect the laws online as they do

offline. "Some governments have internet filters that block mormon.org along with other religious sites. In some cases people still get through, but we are aware of the laws and kindly explain the limitations we have in talking with them," one missionary said. "When someone comes on from Pakistan, we get a prompt from the system indicating that we can answer questions that they have, but we can't invite them to meet with missionaries or attend church."

I asked a friend in Abu Dhabi, where proselytizing is illegal, to log on to missionary chat and see what happened. Rather than the friendly though somewhat generic greeting I received, his chat window said: "Missionaries are not available to chat with you at this time. You may return to Mormon.org to learn more. The chat session has ended."

After a few hours chatting from London, I switched on my virtual private network and instantly relocated my internet protocol address to the United States. Millions of people in countries with internet restrictions use VPNs, proxies and other tools to fake their physical locations and experience an uncensored web.

Knowing this, and assuming missionaries and church officials do too, I was surprised that no one asked where I lived until the end of each conversation, when some politely asked to send missionaries to my home.

I filled out the "request missionary visit" form using my London address and made a fake appointment in Pakistan, which is available in the "select a country" drop-down menu. Both prompted the message: "Thank you for requesting a visit from →

→ The Church of Jesus Christ of Latter-day Saints. You should be contacted by missionaries in a few days." Such contact would presumably be illegal in Pakistan and in many countries.

Eric Hawkins, senior manager of media relations for the church, said these apparent oversights should not be interpreted as foul play. "We go through the front door. We only proselytise where we're formally recognised and welcomed by governments," he said.

In addition to reaching new audiences, online missionary work serves other practical functions. Most Mormons who use missionary chat still spend a majority of their missions offline. Some work online full-time temporarily until they receive a field assignment. For missionaries with physical disabilities, the chat function allows them to serve in ways that would have been impossible until recent years.

Tyson Boardman served at a full-time online mission at the Provo Missionary Training Center in 2009. "Regardless of who you are, you can be an instrument in the Lord's hands," he said in a documentary.

Digital technologies may enhance proselytising, but offline efforts are still necessary. Missionaries I chatted with noted that people couldn't convert to Mormonism online because baptism requires physical contact, according to church doctrine.

Although 76 per cent of missionaries are men, women also spread the gospel online and off. Last year the Mormon Church lowered the minimum age for missionary work from 19 to 18 for men and from 21 to 19 for women. I asked one female missionary: who made the change and why? "God did. It was announced at the general conference by our current prophet Thomas S Monson and we believe it was a revelation from God," she said.

Young missionaries work in teams of two. Women are paired with women and men with men, even online. When I asked why an individual's sex mattered for Missionary Chat, one Mormon said, "those we work with are right next to us. [My partner] is two feet away from me. That way we can talk to each other and make sure we are on the same page."

Missionaries told me what they hoped to accomplish via online chat. One said: "I think it has the potential to be more far-reaching. There are certain individuals that simply will not let people in their homes, but they will gladly participate in an online chat. The world is becoming more reclusive and suspicious of someone knocking on their door. This chat service provides a way for all people with internet access to have their questions answered about the church."

Another added: "I really like that I get to talk to people from all over the world. It is sad that I don't get to see them face-to-face, but I'm so happy that we are using this technology to spread the word of God."

But surely there must be online trolls logging on to start a fight?

"People come here with different intentions. Many are insincere," one missionary said. Another elaborated: "Some come on as a joke, some hoping to argue, but the majority are people who just want to know more. If those we chat with are crude, vulgar, argumentative, we don't hesitate to let them go and invite them to come back later."

I logged on and tried a bit of light theological prodding and spamming to see how the missionaries would react. After trying to engage me for 30 seconds or so, one logged off with "Have a nice day!" Another signed off "God Bless." ☒

© Brian Pellot
www.indexoncensorship.org

Brian Pellot is director of global strategy and religious freedom editor of Religion News Service. He tweets @brianpellot

ABOVE: Uzbek woman studies the Quran at the Ismail Samani Mausoleum, Bukhara, Uzbekistan, 2001

Seizing scriptures

42(4): 69/74 | DOI: 10.1177/0306422013512587

Felix Corley reports on banning Bibles and Qurans in Uzbekistan and the persecution of the people who possess them. Muslims in particular are being given long prison sentences

//UZBEKISTAN – THAT'S the country where they burn Bibles?" a friend of mine remarked to me recently. Indeed it is. And not just Bibles. Forum 18, an NGO that campaigns for religious freedom around the world, has a stack of court verdicts, cases where judges across Uzbekistan have ordered confiscated religious literature, Muslim, Christian, anything, to be destroyed. Despite repeated attempts, we have been unable to discover just what methods the authorities use to destroy such material. Do they shove them in a stove? Chuck them on a bonfire? Maybe they quietly bin them.

Raids on places of worship and the private homes of religious believers almost always end up with religious literature being seized, as well as computers, mobile phones and discs. Then the inevitable cycle begins.

The literature is sent for "expert analysis" to the government's religious affairs committee in the capital, Tashkent. Often, confiscated religious literature must be handed over to "experts" within 24 hours, an incredibly short time for material to travel across potentially long distances. It is then studied carefully, "expert analysis" is typed up and a judgment is made. From

that point on, the literature is classified as illegal, banned, extremist, not suitable for distribution, or whatever other phrase the bureaucrat in charge chooses.

At a trial in November 2012, a Protestant who was fined for possession of "illegal literature" complained to the court about the authenticity of the "expert analysis" used to reach verdicts. The religious affairs committee, he said, was able to read 1,300 books, 2,100 brochures, 450 leaflets, 50 magazines, watch 200 video cassette tapes, listen to 350 audio tapes and produce two "expert analyses" of them in the course of one day. "This beats the Guinness Book of Records," a local Protestant observed.

Police and other authorities in towns hundreds, if not thousands, of miles away from Tashkent are not even remotely surprised when they are notified of the religious affairs committee's decision. They already know it is open season on religious literature and those who possess it. In 10 years of monitoring religious freedom, I have never come across a case where the committee has ruled that the submitted religious literature was acceptable and approved for distribution. Armed with the "expert analysis", all

prosecutors need to do is decide on the charge: if the person in possession of the material is Muslim, chances are they will be charged with a serious criminal offence. If he or she is a Christian, Jehovah's Witness, Baha'i or non-religious individual, prosecutors will choose from a range of lesser charges, which may nevertheless carry a fine or up to two weeks' imprisonment.

Muslims, who make up the largest of Uzbekistan's religious communities, are being sentenced to long prison terms on a wide range of religion-related criminal charges, including anti-constitutional activity, running an extremist organisation and leading an illegal religious or political group. Determining which of the thousands of Muslim prisoners have been punished for bona fide religious activity is difficult. In all likelihood, even the authorities probably cannot tell who is guilty and who is innocent.

Penalties for unapproved religious literature are also frequent. The Code of Administrative Offences, Article 184, Part 2, bans the "illegal storage, production, import, or distribution of religious materials" into Uzbekistan if it is distributed to "physical persons". The offence is punishable by a fine of between 50 and 150 times the minimum monthly salary in Uzbekistan, and includes "confiscation of the religious materials and the relevant means of their production and distribution".

In some cases, police and prosecutors have used confiscated literature as evidence that an individual has been involved in promoting a particular faith, which is also a crime in Uzbekistan. Violation of the Code of Administrative Offences Article 240, Part 2, which prohibits "proselytism" and "other missionary activity", is also punishable by fines of between 50 and 100 times the minimum monthly salary, or administrative arrest for up to 15 days. Those police officials and prosecutors who are very zealous might choose to charge an individual with both crimes if they so wish.

In September 2013, Forum 18 asked Begzod Kadyrov, chief specialist of the government's religious affairs committee in Tashkent and the frequent author of condemnatory "expert analyses", why penalties are handed down for the possession of religious material. Even possession of legal material can be risky: under the country's Religion Law, people are forbidden from keeping religious texts like the Quran or the Bible in their homes. Kadyrov defended the widespread fines, stating that "religious books are only allowed to be read within registered religious communities' buildings".

In the last few years, this has led individuals, Muslims, Christians and others, to dispose of any religious literature they have had in their homes because such literature

This has led to individuals, Muslims, Christians, and others, to dispose of any religious literature they have in their homes

is just too dangerous to own. Some have taken their Qurans and Bibles to their place of worship, hoping that this will save their scriptures from being seized and destroyed. Others have even, however reluctantly and tearfully, chosen to destroy them themselves as a precautionary measure.

Making registered religious buildings a comparatively "safe zone" for religious literature raises another problem. What if you are one of the many religious communities denied the compulsory state registration and thus unable to exist legally? These communities are denied a place of worship and, therefore, forbidden from possessing religious literature. Jehovah's Witnesses are denied legal status everywhere except in Chirchik, a town in Tashkent region. As they are repeatedly reminded, Jehovah's →

→ Witnesses are banned from conducting any religious activity elsewhere.

Yet it is not just religious literature in print that suffers in Uzbekistan. Very few people or organisations are allowed to operate websites covering religious issues. In August, the government claimed the Russian Orthodox diocese website had not registered as a media outlet as required by law, and forced the website to be taken down. A couple of weeks later, after substantial coverage by the foreign media, the website was restored. Religious-themed websites based outside of the country are often blocked, just as independent news, human rights and opposition sites are. For many years, a Russian-based religious news website, portal-credo.ru, was blocked, as was the religious supplement of Russia's newspaper

Those who discuss their faith openly risk imprisonment

Nezavisimaya Gazeta. Two websites belonging to Tajikistan's Islamic Renaissance Party, the only religiously inspired political party tolerated anywhere in Central Asia), continues to be blocked.

Speaking about religious belief is also affected, as part of the ban on "proselytism" and "missionary activity" under Article 5 of the Religion Law. Those who discuss their faith openly risk imprisonment. Breaching Article 216-2 of the criminal code carries a maximum three-year prison term. This article of the criminal code was one of several used against devout Muslim Khayrullo Tursunov, who was extradited back to his native Uzbekistan from Kazakhstan in March 2013 against the express wishes of the UN Committee Against Torture. In June 2013 he was given a 15-year jail sentence for "extremist" exercise of freedom of religion or belief.

Pioneer censor

Uzbekistan was the second former Soviet republic to impose compulsory state registration on all religious communities in the 1990s, following the example of its neighbour Turkmenistan. As state pressure on all religious activity ratcheted up, Uzbekistan was the pioneer in formalising the prior compulsory state censorship of all literature on religious themes published in, printed in or imported into the country in whatever language. Censors check all prayer books and theological tomes coming into the country, including material published in Arabic, Hebrew, Latin, Polish, Armenian, Sanskrit and German.

The bureaucrats never stop. In July, President Islam Karimov ordered the religious affairs committee, the Justice Ministry, the Culture and Sport Ministry, and Publication and Information Agency to prepare a new Rule on the Procedure for Conducting Expert Analysis of Religious Literature Published Abroad. The new rule will not improve the current situation as books on religion are routinely confiscated from individuals returning to Uzbekistan across land borders or at airports. Fines often follow.

The International Post Office in Tashkent routinely opens parcels of religious books and magazines sent from abroad, sending examples to the religious affairs committee, which decides whether to destroy the literature or return it to the sender.

In a discussion with Forum 18 in October 2011, Customs Inspector Dilshod Sadykov estimated that, over the previous year, eight or nine out of every 10 confiscated religious books a-were Muslim. At the time of the interview, he had co-signed a letter to local Baptists explaining why 23 religious books sent by friends in Kazakhstan could not be delivered. (The would-be recipient was, however, allowed to receive the empty box).

Yet as recent cases show, authorities are coming down hard not only on newly-produced or imported religious literature. They are also gunning for literature people have owned for some time. Retrospective censorship, if you like.

In April 2011, police seized the private library of a Tashkent woman's deceased father, including three rare historic editions of the Bible. The religious affairs committee said they contained nothing harmful to the state, but were not to be used to teach religion to children. A judge, who also handed down fines, ordered the books to be destroyed. "This means that he is destroying Bibles that represent the sacred primary source of one of the world's major religions," the woman's father-in-law, Vladimir Shinkin, complained in outrage to some of Uzbekistan's senior government politicians. He got no response.

Under Uzbekistan's constitution, "everyone shall be guaranteed freedom of thought, speech and convictions". It further states that "everyone shall have the right to seek, obtain and disseminate any information, except that which is directed against the existing constitutional system and in some other instances specified by law." But when historic scriptures are no longer safe from destruction, and individuals are punished for the books on religion that they have in their own homes, it is hard to believe this. ☒

©Felix Corley
www.indexoncensorship.org

Felix Corley is editor of Forum 18 News Service, www.forum18.org, which campaigns on and promotes freedom of religion around the world

Religious censorship in Central Asia

There is nowhere in Central Asia where religious literature can be freely published, imported and distributed. Turkmenistan, Tajikistan and Kyrgyzstan all have controls and punishments in place.

Kazakhstan not only introduced full prior compulsory censorship of religious literature, but also bookshop licensing in the October 2011 Religion Law amendments. This is effectively a ban on selling religious literature anywhere else. Asked by Forum 18 in February why people must ask for permission from the authorities before they can sell religious literature, Yerlan Kalmakov of the Kostanai Regional Internal Policy Department, replied, "Imagine what could happen if we allow just anybody to distribute religious materials."

Violating the procedure for importing, publishing or distributing religious literature and materials is subject to administrative punishment. Dozens of such fines were handed down in 2013. Two court orders to destroy confiscated religious books including Bibles and the like were overturned, the second after a public outcry. Independent journalist Sergei Duvanov expressed outrage, pointing out that it put Kazakhstan "on a par with the inquisition of the Middle Ages".

Even more disturbingly, atheist Aleksandr Kharlamov is being prosecuted for expressing his views on religion in his private writings. "This obscurantism on the part of the state is a cause of fear," fellow atheist Duvanov told Forum 18.

In other former Soviet countries outside Central Asia, state censorship of literature on religion is also the norm. Azerbaijan imposes full compulsory prior censorship. Not only do people need permission for a title to be printed or imported, they also need approval for the quantity. Officials routinely limit the print run, if they allow the request at all. Indeed, in a ratcheting up of state censorship, religion law revisions in 2009 required state permission for any shop wanting to sell religious literature or other religious items.

©Felix Corley

Rich Mix is a proudly independent three-screen cinema, multi-arts venue and charitable foundation at the heart of East London.

Live Music
Comedy
Spoken Word
Theatre
Family Events
Documentary &
Independent Film

Every penny of our profit is reinvested in creative learning and community activities and supporting emerging artists.

Last year, we provided local artists with free rehearsal space worth £200,000. Of our 400 cultural events, roughly one third were completely free to attend.

Rich Mix is also home to over 20 creative businesses, employing 300 people.

Become a Rich Mix Member and support our work. For just £30 (individual, £45 joint) you'll get two free cinema tickets and discounted tickets for all films and live cultural events, plus great savings with our partners. For full details see www.richmix.org.uk/membership.

www.richmix.org.uk | 020 7613 7498
35-47 Bethnal Green Road, E1 6LA

Supported by
**ARTS COUNCIL
ENGLAND**

BENI NE DOKTOR
AVUKAZAR MIMA
MÜHENDISLER IST
HEPSI GÖZ ALTIN
#Diren ZMMO

ABOVE: Demonstrators shout slogans as they clash with riot police on Istiklal Street in central Istanbul in July 2013

IN FOCUS

In this section

Changing the rules of the end game

42(4): 78/82 | DOI: 10.1177/0306422013512567

Radical young developers are challenging tired old formulas that have dominated the games industry for years, says **Jason DaPonte**. And some of them are starting debates about some of today's big issues, not just about who can shoot who fastest

IN THE WAKE of this autumn's launch of Grand Theft Auto V, an upgrade of one of the world's best-selling and most controversial video games, you might think that computer games are all about teenage boys glued to their consoles, hypnotised by the fantasy of playing the character of a macho killer protagonist who commits ultra-violent crimes and rescues scantily-clad babes-in-distress. If you've not seen the hype, games probably mean the rather less disturbing picture of children mesmerised and wasting hours on the sofa in front of the screen when they should be doing something else. But not all games are violent fantasies or brain-numbing diversions. My company recently launched a Facebook game, Meet the World Brain (http://on.fb.me/H37mxZ), which encourages young people to think about the corporate control of knowledge and data. It was designed to promote Ben Lewis's documentary Google and the World Brain, nominated for a prize at the Sundance film festival for independent movies, which covers the same themes but targets a very different audience.

Computer games and censorship

Games are subject to government censorship around the world. Various industry boards exist to regulate and provide ratings for the console-games industry, much as they do for films. However, the level to which the Apple App Store censors mobile games is perhaps less well known.

"Apple is known for banning games that aim to address socio-political themes or current events," says Asi Burak, who heads the network Games for Change. Endgame: Syria (http://game-thenews.net/index.php/endgame-syria/) from the UK-based alternative games creator Game The News (a member of Games for Change) was banned by Apple but is now available on the web. The game examines the complexities of the Syrian civil war through card-based gameplay from the perspective of the Syrian rebels. The consequences of players' choices, all of which have an impact on the outcome, are outlined by the game, showing the options available to the Syrian rebels and the long and difficult road to potential war resolution.

"We view apps differently than books or songs, which we do not curate. If you want to

Games that deal with serious subjects are not part of the mainstream. Like Hollywood, the console-games industry prefers to stick with entertainment that appeals to wide audiences. Given that many console games now cost more than films to produce, this probably makes commercial sense.

Outside the mainstream industry, on open platforms, there are a number of games that take on more serious subject matters, including several that address questions of freedom of expression, as well as censorship. The "open web" – a section of the internet accessible to everyone and where the emphasis is on open source software and wider access to technologies – is cheaper for developers to use. Compared to console games, the same is true of mobile networks, popular proprietary online environments such as Facebook, and "virtual-world" 3D games such as Second Life, so these platforms are increasingly used to explore some of today's most controversial and difficult topics.

"Some issues are easily disguised in games – women in action, historical points of view, free will – and it is great that gamers can play around with these ideas," says Mia Bennett, a game publisher who runs businesses in the UK and Iran.

Gone Gitmo and Wall Jumpers, created by Nonny de la Peña and Peggy Weil, use Second Life to take players into places the media cannot reach. In Gone Gitmo (http://gonegitmo.blogspot.co.uk/), interviews with ex-prisoners were used to recreate the Guantanamo Bay camp in virtual space. Players put on an orange prisoner jumpsuit and are transported as prisoners on a plane into the camp, where they are confronted by a place in which no cameras are allowed – but they

Some issues are easily disguised in games – women in action, historical points of view, free will – and it is great that gamers can play around with these ideas

can hear and see the stories of some of the prisoners. Walljumpers (http://archive.org/details/Walljumpers) takes a more light-hearted approach by letting users virtually jump over the most dangerous borders in the world, which is great fun if you've ever wanted to catapult yourself from South to North Korea or vice versa.

De la Peña's current project was inspired by camera-phone footage of US police →

criticise a religion, write a book. If you want to describe sex, write a book or a song, or create a medical app," the App-Store guidelines state, clearly showing that Apple thinks it can exert more control over games than other media.

Apple's guidelines are problematic, however. The criteria used are not clear and are applied without consistency when games are submitted for technical review, largely by technical testers and not by content experts. One developer who asked not to be named said that he was forced to remove a Hitler character from an educational history game about World War II because it might be viewed as encouraging neo-Nazism.

MolleIndustria's Phone Story educational game, which looks at the dark side of smartphone technology development, was banned by Apple and its website now boasts a "Banned from the AppStore" badge instead of an "Available on the AppStore" logo.

Stupid decisions by gatekeepers applying guidelines crudely lead to poor-quality content being distributed to audiences: they do not protect them. Google Play is the AppStore's main competitor and is far more permissive of controversial content, with very few reports of game banning. ⊠

ABOVE: Images from the game Walljumpers by Peggy Weil and Nonny de la Peña

→ officers using force at a crime scene – footage they tried to delete. "Use of Force Protocol is based on mobile phone audio and video captured by two bystanders who became witnesses to the homicide of a migrant by more than a dozen US border patrol agents," she says. The new game's development is funded by the Tribeca Film Institute and an AP/Google Technology and Journalism grant.

"When the episode escalated, two border patrol agents grabbed mobile phones from bystanders and began erasing video material – but two witnesses managed to slip away. My source says that one of the agents was trained to work with a variety of mobiles so that he was expert in erasing material on any phone he would come across. My intent for project is to show how important it is that we stop that kind of censorship. The border patrol's report on the death was a complete whitewash."

Developers with controversial stories to tell use game mechanics and platforms to engage players – but then surprise them by subverting their expectations. MolleIndustria, an independent Italian developer (http://www.molleindustria.org/), made headlines with Desert of Real, which subverted the US army recruitment game America's Army. The game depicts how soldiers as often lonely and suffering the consequences of post-traumatic stress disorder. The same studio released Operation Paedo-Priest, in which players have to cover up sex scandals on behalf of the church.

Games For Change (http://www.gamesforchange.org) is an international network set up in 2012 that showcases games that promote social and political change. Several directly address human rights, including freedom of expression. On The Ground Reporter Darfur puts the player in the shoes of a journalist in Sudan who has to uncover the truth. The developers are currently discussing creating a series of "on the ground journalist" games that can sit alongside "first person shooter" games as a popular genre.

Games For Change has also released a Half the Sky Movement – The Game (https://www.facebook.com/HalftheGame), which aims to encourage social action for global gender equality. It has built a user-base of more than one million players since its release earlier in early 2013.

Players are tasked with selecting and printing only stories that will maintain social order

Lucas Pope, an independent games developer, tackles the issue of censorship head on with The Republia Times (http://dukope.com/play.php?g=trt). In this simple game, the user is put in the chair of the editor-in-chief of a newspaper run by the fictional Ministry of Media for the fictional nation of Republia. Players are tasked with selecting and printing only stories that will maintain social order and a positive image of the nation.

There are even a few mainstream console games that cut against the grain. Although it relies on "first person shooter" formula for much of its play, The Bioshock Infinite game (http://www.bioshockinfinite.com) uses propaganda from church and state in the US as a backdrop throughout.

Radical games are often controversial. In Pipe Trouble (http://pipetrouble.com), a game from Pop Sandbox Productions funded by the public service broadcaster TVOntario (TVO), players have to build an oil pipeline, balancing such factors as damage to the environment, profitability and avoiding problems with eco-terrorists. The presence of eco-terrorist enemy characters in the game caused a media storm in Canada – and even the government pitched in to say that it glamourised eco-terrorism. It was sub- →

→ sequently pulled from the TVO website, though an independent review later exonerated the game.

Radical games developers are supporting freedom of expression – but they face several challenges. Knee-jerk reactions from non-gamers, media misrepresentation of games culture and risk-averse games publishers could all threaten their distribution.

Fortunately, the open web provides direct-to-audience distribution, which will generally provide a channel for games developers who are willing and able to distribute their own games, even where they cannot get their stories onto console gaming platforms. Independent radical games are starting to have a real impact – the usage stats for some of them are encouraging and the film industry is starting to take notice. (Pipe Trouble was featured at the Cannes Film Festival.) It's going to be an uphill battle, but it's one worth fighting. ☒

© Jason DaPonte
www.indexoncensorship.org

Jason DaPonte is managing director of The Swarm and former editor for BBC Mobile.

An Uncertain Glory

JEAN DRÈZE & AMARTYA SEN

'A major work by two of the world's
most perceptive and intelligent
India-watchers writing today'

William Dalrymple, *New Statesman*

OUT NOW

ALLEN
LANE

YES WE SCAN.

DEAL WITH IT.

UNITED WE PROGRESS TOWARD A PERFECTLY MONITORED SOCIETY

ABOVE: Protests against NSA surveillance, Frankfurt, 27 September 2013

A net of our own?

||||||||||||||||||||||||||||||||||||||||||||||||||||

42(4): 84/88 | DOI: 10.1177/0306422013512967

The scandal over US surveillance of the internet has led to a bizarre wave of cyber-nationalism in Germany, says **Sally Gimson**

DEUTSCHE TELEKOM, GERMANY'S national telecommunications giant, is working on a "national internet" to replace the present American-dominated system. It made the little-noticed announcement in October, a few weeks after the German general election. It says that a national internet will mean that emails and data will be transmitted only through German lines within Germany's borders. The catchy slogan is "national routing".

"The idea is that, contrary to today's common practice, data from a German sender to a German recipient will not be sent through another country," said Philipp Blank, Deutsche Telekom's spokesman. He suggested that this national internet could ultimately be expanded to cover all the European countries that have signed up to the Schengen agreement on open borders.

Expert commentators are sceptical about the desire to keep the internet within national borders. They point out not only that it would be impracticable but that it is the model that dictatorships use.

Professor Niko Härting, a Berlin lawyer who specialises in internet law, says: "When Iran says it is building an Iranian →

→ internet we all say this is dictatorship. The more closed a system, the more easily it can be monitored."

Yet German politicians have given a nod and a wink to the idea.

The reason for this sudden interest in keeping data from the outside world is obvious: the exposure by the American whistleblower Edward Snowden of the extensive monitoring of email and internet usage all over the world by the US National Security Agency (NSA), closely aided by Britain's Government Communications Headquarters (GCHQ).

Across Europe the story has perhaps had the greatest impact in Germany. The weekly magazine Der Spiegel has worked closely on

In left-wing kindergartens in Berlin, six-year-olds are learning about the bravery of Edward Snowden

Snowden's material with the Guardian in London, publishing new revelations issue-by-issue. It estimates that the NSA has been recording up to 60 million German metadata connections per day, with millions of emails intercepted, items of data copied and phone calls recorded. It seems that Germany is the European country under closest scrutiny by the US and Britain – although, the NSA records also show that Germany counts only as a middle-ranking country for surveillance.

Der Spiegel has been unrelenting in its coverage. Jakob Augstein, whose father Rudolf founded the magazine in 1947, used its pages to express his outrage at the "humiliation" and "powerlessness" exposed by Snowden's revelations. "Once you get past all the rhetoric, what is the actual issue we're dealing with here?" he asked in an editorial. "The United States has massively and systematically violated the civil rights of people who have no possibility of voting

against its practices in elections. After all, the NSA and CIA and whatever the other organisations are called aren't operating under German laws when they're supposedly protecting the security of the free world."

In August the controversy briefly threatened to derail Chancellor Angela Merkel's re-election campaign. During the sole television debate between her and her Social Democrat challenger Peer Steinbrück, her only sticky moment came when she was asked about the NSA. Her reply typified the stonewalling that has been the German government's preferred line. She said that she had no reason not to trust what the NSA and the American government had told her, and that no German law had been infringed. Nevertheless, she would gladly talk to the Americans about a data protection treaty.

The opposition Greens and Social Democrats belatedly and half-heartedly tried to get a debate on the issue in the Bundestag in the last sitting before the election, but were not successful. The leader of Merkel's Christian Democratic Union in the Bundestag, Michael Grosse-Brömer, said there was "no evidence of mass surveillance" of German citizens and that the opposition had no interest in serious debate: they were simply "trying to make a scandal out of a subject where there is no scandal" for electoral purposes.

But if Merkel and her allies – and some of her opponents – hoped that the story would disappear after the election, they were soon disappointed. Within a month of her victory in September, Der Spiegel reported that German intelligence sources had raised the possibility that Merkel's mobile phone had been tapped by the NSA. The story was sufficiently plausible for her to call US President Barack Obama personally to demand an explanation.

Many Germans have been deeply distressed by the exposure of American and British surveillance, with opinion polls showing strong support for Snowden. This is partly explicable by Germany's 20th century history.

The East German Stasi had files on almost everyone in the country, and the Nazis used their security services and the Gestapo to terrorise the population.

But what appears to have angered Germans in the current scandal is the part played by the Americans and the British. It feeds into a German narrative of American occupation, about which there has been ambivalence since the end of the second world war. During the Cold War, West Germany needed American and British Nato forces on its soil to protect it against the Soviet Union. But this military presence was also evidence that the Germans did not have true sovereignty.

The left was particularly disturbed by American nuclear weapons in Germany, concerned that the country might be reduced to a battlefield between the two great superpowers, the US and Russia. In the early 1980s, walls all over West Germany were daubed with the slogan "Petting not Pershing", a version of "Make love not war" referring to American Pershing II intermediate-range nuclear missiles, controlled by the Americans but based at three sites in West Germany.

Today, with the Cold War long over, graffiti on buildings in Berlin read "©Google", a reference to Google Street View. Google Street View has been repeatedly challenged through the German courts for invasion of privacy. If you use Street View to look at German cities, you see a remarkable number of buildings blurred out. Their owners have gone through the time-consuming process of getting Google to agree to respect their privacy.

Matthew Tempest, a British journalist in Berlin, says that even before the NSA scandal Germans were prone to use anonymous profiles on Facebook, refuse to save their documents on Google docs and choose German webmail services rather than American ones. Whereas in Britain it is now possible to follow every twist and turn of national politics through Twitter, it is just not used in the same way by German journalists or politicians.

Since the NSA affair broke, the suspicion of large American internet and IT companies has increased. Tempest says that in left-wing kindergartens in Berlin, six-year-olds are learning about the bravery of Edward Snowden in defying the NSA.

With American dominance of the IT industry now widely seen by Germans as a form of cyber-occupation by a foreign power, it is no surprise that large German telecommunications companies have seen a commercial opportunity to exploit this distrust.

"The Germans don't care about snooping as long as it isn't the Americans who are doing it"

Niko Härting says: "I am convinced that anti-American feeling is behind the German reaction. I have heard the same people who are making the most outraged comments about NSA spying being quite mild about the activities of our own secret service."

He says that Germans have seemed perfectly happy to have the Bundesnachrichtendienst (BND) read their emails. There was barely an outcry when a German parliamentary committee discovered that in 2010 the BND had read 37 million emails, identified through key words like "bomb", without any judicial oversight of their activities.

"All they have to do is to walk into Angela Merkel's office and ask for permission to search for certain key words," says Härting. "And we don't really know what they do."

Härting is certain that at least some of the BND's activities are illegal under the German constitution, but so far the agency has not been challenged. It is difficult for an individual to challenge it, he explains, because that individual would have to →

→ prove that he or she had been targeted – and people do not know if their own emails have been read.

The politicians, he says, could challenge it, but no political party has an interest in doing so.

"The Germans don't care about snooping as long as it isn't the Americans who are doing it," he says.

That is why the idea of a German internet is attractive. It may well be unrealistic, but it addresses Germans' fears that they are being occupied by a foreign power and gives them some sense that they are taking control over their own affairs.

Young Germans say nervously that the proposal is silly, that German companies do not have the technology and expertise to develop impenetrable IT systems, and that they will be forced to use American technology whether they like it or not.

The real problem, however, is that, scarred in the 20th century by the Stasi and the Nazi secret service, Germany is turning in on itself and refusing to have a public debate about why it feels so angry about American and British surveillance of its emails and data.

"There is no debate about this," says Tilman Fichter. "Germany does not think it is strong enough to have the debate. People want to solve the problem in a technical way because they cannot solve it in political way. Germany feels economically strong, but not politically powerful." ☒

©Sally Gimson
www.indexoncensorship.org

Sally Gimson is former freelance Berlin correspondent for the Sunday Times and news producer at Deutsche Welle TV.

Protest posted

42(4): 89/91 | DOI: 10.1177/0306422013512964

After thousands of people went on to the streets of Addis Ababa to protest earlier this year, there was a hope that dissenting voices might be heard again in Ethiopia. But, finds **Philippa McIntyre**, those who report on government failures continue to face arrest and accusations of terrorism

WHEN PIONEER JOURNALIST Muluken Tesfaw found himself in a police cell, he realised just how dangerous the situation is for journalists in today's Ethiopia. He had been arrested for investigating the illegal land evictions of a minority group living near the Grand Ethiopian Renaissance Dam.

Tesfaw, who works for privately-owned weekly newspaper Ethio-Mihdar, was reporting extensively on the eviction of thousands of Amhara people, some of whom were injured or killed when their homes and farms were burnt down by authorities in May 2013. After interviewing villagers and photographing burnt-out buildings, local government officials arrested the journalist, tied him up, and moved him to various police cells in the region, some with no access to toilet facilities. He was taken to the regional government 360km away for questioning, accused of acts of terrorism and held for eight days without charge.

He believes that the situation for journalists like him, who are working to expose the government's actions, is unlikely to improve any time soon. "The police commissioner told the regional government that they had detained a terrorist," he said. "I tried to convince him that I am not a terrorist and that I am working for the wellness of my country. But he intimidated me."

They released Tesfaw without charge. In a breach of his constitutional rights, authorities gave no reason for his arrest, and confiscated the evidence he had gathered from the evictions. He wrote the articles from memory in spite of his imprisonment.

"While there are enough spaces at Kaliti and Maekelawi prisons, the imprisonment of journalists and politicians will continue," he says. He is certain other newspapers and media organisations will face closure in the near future. Unless the system put in place by the Ethiopian People's Revolutionary Democratic Front (EPRDF) "is changed by a miracle, things will get worse," he adds. Although he has not faced any direct attacks since May, he believes he is still at risk. "Here in Ethiopia, the ruling party looks at private journalists like they are opposition parties," he says.

Earlier this year, there was a glimmer of hope for press freedom in the country when 15,000 people marched through the centre of Addis Ababa to demand the release of jailed journalists and political prisoners. This was a significant moment, according to news reports. Aside from some smaller →

ABOVE: A news conference held by the Unity for Democracy and Justice Party. The party called on the government to scrap the anti-terrorism law, which has been widely used to stifle dissent, Addis Ababa, 20 June 2013

→ protests by Muslim groups, the march was the first major demonstration since violent election protests in 2005 when hundreds of people were killed or imprisoned by government forces.

More significant was the fact that the new prime minister and leader of EPRDF, Hailemariam Desalegn, who came to power last year after long-time leader Mele Zenawi

Even though the internet is heavily censored, they are still working to find a way

died suddenly, apparently allowed the event to take place. The demonstration, led by new opposition group, the Blue Party, passed peacefully.

For a moment at least, critics seemed hopeful that this apparent openness to public dissent was a sign that the new leadership might allow space for other voices in the debate. Another similar protest took place

in September, this time led by opposition party Unity for Democracy and Justice. Had these two events revealed a shift in the political climate?

Like many of his peers, Muluken is adamant that there will be no change under the new leader. "I strongly believe that the late prime minister is ruling and managing the party and Ethiopia from the grave. As long as the new prime minister does not have his own dreams and visions, how can the political system change? His advisers are the same people as before."

The ongoing situation for journalists in the country appears to support his argument. The detention of journalists who criticise the government's actions, or are perceived to do so, remains increasingly common. Ethiopia is close to becoming the top jailor of journalists in Africa, overtaking Eritrea. The situation for those in prison is extremely serious. Human Rights Watch published a shocking report in October on the torture and ill treatment faced by prisoners in Maekelawi jail, where scores of journalists are held.

Campaigners around the world are currently fighting for the release of outspoken journalists Reeyot Alemu, winner of the 2013 UNESCO/Guillermo Cano press freedom prize, and Eskinder Nega, detained since 2011 for alleged "links with terrorist organisations and conspiracy to harm national security". They are being held under the widely used 2009 Anti-Terrorism Act, and are facing up to 14 years behind bars.

According to the Committee for the Protection of Jourrnalists (CPJ), 49 journalists have fled Ethiopia since 2007. Fasil Aragaw is one such journalist from Ethiopia currently living in exile. He previously worked for the state-run Ethiopian Radio and Television Agency, but after the 2005 elections, he explains, the government recruited "gatekeepers" for the most influential editorial positions. They censored everything he wrote, and he could no longer exercise freedom of expression as a professional journalist. He resigned, and joined Transparency International Ethiopia, where he worked on issues linked to investigative journalism and anti-corruption. He started a blog on press issues, but after publishing just eight articles, it was blocked. He was put under government surveillance and, in fear of arrest, he fled to Kenya where he now lives in exile.

"Being a critical journalist in Ethiopia, there is always the risk of being jailed. Even after I came to Kenya I feared the government security officers might take me back and arrest me," he says.

While Aragaw commends the opposition parties for holding protests, he does not believe they will make any difference. The prime minister, he says, recently told local journalists that public protests will not be allowed to take place in future unless the opposition starts making different demands. What the prime minister means, he says, is that the opposition make demands that are not about anti-terror laws.

"There is no change regarding lack of press freedom in Ethiopia. There should be political willingness from the top level of the government, and press freedom laws should be amended in order to fit with international standards. There must be a general political change to see a good press in Ethiopia."

As well as censoring and controlling the print media, last year the government passed a new telecommunications law, hampering online debate, and blocking access to websites which criticised the government. Despite this, Mohamed Keita from the CPJ in New York believes new technology and the determination of journalists and activist groups may offer some hope for the future.

"You have young journalists like Muluken Tesfaw who are still trying to do their jobs under very difficult conditions. You've got the Zone 9 bloggers [a group of Ethiopian bloggers who are concerned about human rights and democratisation] trying to use social media to contribute local, independent or alternative perspectives to developments on the ground. Even the peaceful Muslim demonstrators were using social media very creatively to circumvent the government's efforts to suppress news about the protests."

He adds, "Even though the internet is heavily censored, they were still working to find a way. There is the general idea that people are constantly fighting or trying to counter censorship."

Over the next year, in the run up to the elections in 2015, we will see how protest and social media contribute to the campaign for press freedom by bringing the issue to the attention of the international community. Perhaps then the Ethiopian government will finally be forced to take note. 図

©Philippa McIntyre
www.indexoncensorship.org

Philippa McIntyre is a media consultant and ran community sports programmes for street children in Ethiopia with the charity Football Action

Rise of Turkish citizens' media

42(4): 92/95 | DOI: 10.1177/0306422013511563

When grassroots protesters flocked to Gezi Park, the bias and moral bankruptcy of Turkey's mainstream media was blatantly exposed. The public started to turn to a new type of media outlet for their news, while big media broadcast cooking shows and animal documentaries, writes journalist and commentator **Kaya Genç**

WHEN REPORTER AYÇA Söylemez witnessed a group of heavily armed riot police beating a protester outside the headquarters of Bianet, an alternative news outlet where she has worked for the past two years, she did her best to report the event, just as any decent reporter would have done. Bianet published her article, while mainstream news outlets broadcast cookery programmes and the Turkish edition of CNN showed a (now infamous) documentary about the habits of penguins. The penguin documentary quickly became a symbol of just how dramatically the mainstream media was ignoring the real stories.

Söylemez and I shared a deep sense of shock: Bianet's office just happens to be between my own apartment and Orhan Pamuk's Museum of Innocence in Çukurcuma, also home to dozens of antique shops, giving the neighbourhood a silent, peaceful quality. Until the governor of Istanbul banned May Day celebrations in Taksim earlier this year, the street had almost never seen any political activity.

Had Söylemez worked for a big news organisation, her report would probably have never see the light of day. But thanks to new web and print publications springing up in the country, offering alternatives to the mainstream press, her journalism found an important audience.

I met her one morning in September at the offices of Bianet (an acronym for "Bağımsız İletişim Ağı" or "the Independent News Network"), where she works alongside a ten-strong team of reporters and editors. The Bianet project started in 1997, when representatives of small local papers and television stations convened in Ankara to discuss whether they could have a grassroots approach to the business of covering news without the intervention of large companies with elaborate connections to the state. After Bianet's website was launched in 2000, columnists from the mainstream newspapers angrily denounced it. They portrayed Bianet as a sinister force trying to destroy the country's official narrative. At the time, the leading trio of mainstream papers, Hürriyet, Milliyet and Sabah carefully managed the political conversation. The voices of human rights advocates, Kurds, socialists and conservatives were

expertly suppressed or pushed to the margins of public discourse.

Today, 13 years after they launched the website and two months after Turkish media's problematic coverage of political protests in Istanbul's Gezi Park, Turkish people are increasingly relying on networks like Bianet and reporters like Söylemez. "Sell bagels instead, at least you'll be leading an honourable life!" was one of the most popular slogans among Gezi Park protesters – a refrain addressed not only to riot police but also to media workers employed by mainstream publications.

"Mainstream media executives are not independent from the government, they are competing against each other in order to get government contracts," Söylemez said. "During the Gezi events seven newspapers had the exact same headline — this clearly showed how streamlined the views of the mainstream press had become." As a former employee of numerous mainstream newspapers, Söylemez finds the Bianet experience liberating. Since the Gezi protests, said Söylemez, "our readership has increased seven to eightfold."

Bianet may arguably be one of the best examples of independent, non-profit news outlets in Turkey, but it is certainly not the only one. There are other websites, such as Gerçek Gündem and T24.com.tr, and radio stations like Açık Radyo. They are managed by small editorial teams on modest salaries, and focus on the critical voices that no longer find a place in the mainstream media. "Some of those alternative publications can be identified as 'dissident' or 'leftist' or as representative of the views of the main opposition party," Söylemez said. "What makes Bianet different is its concentration on news production and its independent business model."

Another reporter, Nihan Bora, is among those who migrated to alternative media after spending years working at mainstream publications, including the prestigious Milliyet. Bora currently works for Zete.com,

the brainchild of Nurcan Akad, one of Turkey's most influential editors. "Akad knows how to think outside the box", Bora said. She keeps her eye on the trends in digital publishing, "adapting them to a Turkish environment". The result is a news outlet that avoids the sensationalism of the mainstream press. "You will never see headlines that include phrases like BREAKING! or SHOCKING NEWS! on Zete," Bora said. "We don't use those cliches; we are strongly against the exaggerations of conventional publications. Our style is plain and devoid of those rhetorical ornaments."

In September, I put Bora's claim to the

"If the Gezi Park demonstrations proved anything, it is how badly served the Turkish public is by a partisan and corrupted media"

test. I looked at their coverage of a police raid in Istanbul's Gülsuyu neighbourhood that followed civil unrest over the activities of drugs gangs in the area. Hürriyet's website ran the following headline: "This is not Mexico, this is Istanbul," revealing the news outlet as definitely sensationalist – and more than a little Mexico-phobic. "Massive operation in Istanbul!" roared the headline on the Sabah homepage: it contained little information and plenty of speculation. Zete's headline was simpler and more informative: "Attack on group who protested against drug cartels in their neighborhood leaves one dead."

Bora admits she overlooked the importance of alternative media when she started out in the industry. "I thought I could best learn about journalism if I worked in a mainstream publication", she said. "But I had →

ABOVE: Toy penguins in front of a damaged news van, part of a protest against the mainstream media's failure to cover the Gezi Park protests in May and June 2013. Instead of reporting on the thousands-strong protest, the main TV channels broadcast cookery programmes and a documentary on penguins

→ the chance to observe how both worlds worked. Then I made my decision."

Bora's moment of realisation came during protests in Gezi Park. "It became perfectly clear that we didn't need the mainstream any more," she said. "Those interested in news got it from social media. Citizen journalism thrived. Readers convened around alternative publications that had no choice but to give an accurate view of the events. Otherwise they would lose their readers to other websites or to social media."

Around the time I was interviewing editors and reporters working for alterna-

tive publications, a group of prestigious journalists (all of them former employees of the mainstream press) announced that they had set up an "independent journalism platform" called P24. Headed by the famous Turkish journalist Hasan Cemal, who lost his column in Milliyet this year after the proprietor of the newspaper tried, unsuccessfully, to censor his articles, and then fired him, the platform seeks to improve professional standards in the media and educate reporters and editors about ethics.

When I asked Andrew Finkel, long-time

Turkey correspondent for the New York Times and P24 co-founder, whether those independent new publications could be the future of the Turkish press, he sounded optimistic. "If the Gezi Park demonstrations earlier this year proved anything, it is how badly served the Turkish public is by a partisan and corrupted media", he said. "The refusal of major press organisations to report the events literally on their doorsteps gave pause for thought. People saw how badly their concerns were covered and began to realise that a whole variety of issues (from Kurdish identity politics to environmental issues) were also being spun or glossed over. With the moral bankruptcy of the established media (very much the result of proprietors pursing non-press interests), independently minded media acquired a new status."

Finkel then reminded me of the case of T24.com.tr, which saw its readership (measured in hits) rise from around 30,000 to 50,000 hits per day after Hasan Cemal was fired from Milliyet. Cemal, who is 69, immediately travelled with retreating PKK militants across the Iraqi border, an account of which was serialized on T24.com.tr. The site's readership shot up to 400,000 hits per day in the midst of the Gezi events and has stabilized at between 100,000 and 110,000 visitors.

"Even before Gezi, a group of disaffected journalists in Turkey, of which I count myself one, decided to form P24," Finkel said. "We try to marshal resources to support journalistic independence in Turkey. The theory is you can bend the truth only so far until something snaps."

It seems as if a great number of ethical values have recently been devalued in the country's media. With any luck, alternative media will help to correct this, restoring some of the standards that have in recent years been lost. ☒

© Kaya Genç
www.indexoncensorship.org

Kaya Genç is a journalist novelist and essayist based in Istanbul. His work has appeared in the Paris Review Daily, the Guardian, the Financial Times and the London Review of Books blog. His first novel, L'Avventura (Macera) was published in 2008

Fight club

42(4): 96/98 | DOI: 10.1177/0306422013513534

Andrei Aliaksandrau describes journalist Iryna Khalip's courageous fight for human rights in Belarus, and pays tribute to the award winner

RYNA KHALIP STARTED her journalistic career during the last years of the Soviet Union. She witnessed the changes that the fall of the Berlin Wall and the end of the communist empire brought about. She saw the new hopes those changes inspired; and she watched as those hopes collapsed when Alexander Lukashenko came to power in Belarus in 1994. For these, and all the tough pieces of journalism she has done, against the odds, she has just been presented with the International Writer of Courage 2013 PEN/Pinter Prize, along with playwright Sir Tom Stoppard.

In 1997 Khalip was severely beaten by the police together with her father, the well-known Belarusian playwright and scriptwriter Uladzimir Khalip, during a protest against the union between Russia and Belarus in Minsk. The public prosecutor's office refused to initiate a criminal case against the police officers. It ended up with the journalist being fined for slapping a prosecutor who saw no offence in police brutality.

She worked for leading Belarusian newspapers, including the Belorusskaya Delovaya Gazeta, a Belarusian business newspaper which was closed in 2006 due to the pressure from the authorities. And for years Khalip has been a special reporter in Belarus for the Russian Novaya Gazeta.

Her reporting and firm stand have been recognised both by the professional community and civil society and in different ways by the authorities of the country. The former have garlanded her with numerous national and international journalistic and human rights prizes and awards after the latter subjected her to criminal cases, interrogations and trials.

A new stage of Khalip's life started on the cold night of 19 December 2010. She was in the Independence Square of Minsk beside her husband Andrei Sannikov, an oppositional presidential candidate. She was there to protest against voting fraud and demand free and fair elections. And she faced extreme police brutality again. Protesters were dispersed by the police, hundreds of people were detained and later sentenced for participation in peaceful protest. Khalip was detained as well, as a real journalist, in the line of duty. She was live on her phone to Russian radio giving her report about what happened in Minsk, when the police stopped the car she and Sannikov were in, dragged them out and brought to the KGB prison.

In May 2011, she was given a two-year suspended prison sentence for "participation in mass disturbances". In fact, for two years she lived under house arrest. She was not allowed to leave Minsk, had to be at home by 10pm every day and report to the police weekly. In July 2013 Khalip had her suspended sentence lifted by a Minsk court, but

ABOVE: Journalist Iryna Khalip

did not really accept her freedom as a sign of mercy from the ruling regime.

"They took three years of my life. For two years I lived under de facto house arrest. They should not expect me to thank them for not sending me to prison," Khalip told journalists after the court announced she was free. "There can be no such thing as an 'ex-political prisoner' until this fascist regime is gone in our country," the journalist added.

When Khalip was awarded the International Writer of Courage 2013 PEN/Pinter Prize this autumn, along with playwright Sir Tom Stoppard, it was not a surprise. Tom Stoppard is well known for his writing, and for his campaigning for freedom in Belarus.

Stoppard: Anyone who meets her must be struck by her energy and vivacity, and by her dedication

And Iryna Khalip is renowned for a courage that goes far beyond her writing.

Stoppard told Index: "I met Irina Khalip in Minsk eight years ago. The political and →

→ civic climate was bad then but it is much worse now, especially for a brave independent voice like Irina's. Anyone who meets her must be struck by her energy and vivacity, and by her dedication. I was proud to share the PEN/Pinter Prize with her a few weeks ago."

Her work is much acknowledged for its impact, and overcoming obstacles. Zhanna Litvina, chair of the Belarusian Association of Journalists, the leading independent organisation for journalists in the country, said: "Iryna is an extremely talented person beyond any doubt. Moreover, she shows what happens when talent comes together with the determination to take a firm stand. She is a political journalist, who is intolerant of any injustice, sometimes even morbidly intolerant. I really adore her being so firm in her views and beliefs despite all terrible ordeals she has undergone. Iryna definitely sees Belarus as a democratic country where people can live without fear; and her determination and hope inspires the people who surround her."

And Khalip stays determined, because nothing can change her belief what she is doing is right. She says she is not leaving Belarus, because it is her country, and she wants it to be free and democratic. She wants to see Belarusian people in charge of their future with no fear, but with their rights and freedoms respected.

And she keeps writing with the courage she is known for. ☒

©Andrei Aliaksandrau
www.indexoncensorship.org

Andrei Aliaksandrau is Belarus and OSCE programme office at Index, and a Belarusian journalist

Muckrakers synonymous

42(4): 99/102 | DOI: 10.1177/0306422013513536

Investigative reporter Eric Schlosser talks to **Rachael Jolley** about the future of journalism, muckraking, the Snowden saga and the importance of cracking censorship

THERE AREN'T MANY books that change attitudes, but Eric Schlosser's Fast Food Nation was one of them. The questions it raised about what we eat, where it comes from and how fast food chains make their money had an extraordinary public impact. It made a large group of people who had never worried before about the food industry think seriously about it. And it was turned into a film.

He did what many journalists aspire to do but find it increasingly difficult to achieve; write something that challenges public attitudes, or pressurises a government to change a law.

But Schlosser says that what inspired him to write Fast Food Nation was not a desire to make people worry about what they put in their stomachs, but an urge to highlight the plight of people working in the food industry.

There is an echo here of the author Upton Sinclair, whose fictionalised expose of the Chicago meat-packing industry, The Jungle, was published in 1906. Sinclair's novel was a massive success. It helped create the public pressure that led to the Meat Inspection Act and an early incarnation of the Food and Drug Administration. But Sinclair said he was disappointed that the public focused

on food, not the plight of the workers, after reading his book.

Schlosser says Sinclair is one of his heroes, and that's not surprising. Schlosser has a lot in common with the early 20th-century "muckrakers" whose forensic work dug out detail and stories that left the public horrified. And the link to Sinclair doesn't end with Fast Food Nation; Schlosser was executive producer on Paul Thomas Anderson's film There Will Be Blood, starring Daniel Day-Lewis, which is based on Sinclair's Oil.

Schlosser's new book, Command and Control, is on a very different topic: the history of nuclear weapons. But his approach is familiar. He is a detail geek, nothing if not persistent. The endnotes stretch to nearly 100 pages, which would not be out of place in an academic textbook. He conducted no fewer than 100 interviews with people about an accident involving a Titan II intercontinental ballistic missile near Damascus, Arkansas, that came close to disaster.

He says he has spent so long working on food and nuclear weapons because both stories are about unaccountable power and safety. "In writing about nuclear weapons, it's a similar story about power – bureaucratic institutions that wield enormous influence, →

ABOVE: One of the highpoints of investigative journalism, the Washington Post's Watergate reports. Here former Attorney General John Mitchell takes the witness stand

Credit: CSU Archives/Everett Collection/Alamy

→ whose operations are largely in secret and are fundamentally undemocratic."

He spent six years researching Command and Control. How could he afford that? He says that after the film of Fast Food Nation he got a decent advance, and that he was lucky. "There's so much less support today for investigative journalism than before," he says. "My role as a journalist has been an old-fashioned notion of exposing injustices, of exposing the workings of powerful institutions in the belief that this knowledge is essential to democracy and that people deserve to have it."

Command and Control appears at a time when the debate about investigative journalism and national security is dominated by the story of the whistleblower Edward Snowden. Schlosser has considered the implications. He says that an unnamed expert, with high security clearance, read a draft of the book and advised whether any detail could expose or harm the defence of the US. His motive for publishing, he adds, was to get the US government to make a clearer assessment of the risks of owning nuclear weaponry, and to be able to learn from earlier mistakes.

Schlosser says that the Titan II incident in Damascus, Arkansas, could have helped inform decisions afterwards. "What is most concerning to me is the lies that were constant through the Cold War were that there was no risk of an accidental detonation, that there was no risk of a weapon being stolen, that there was no risk of our own personnel using our weapons without permission. Those were lies."

He says: "Again and again, what had been censored was information that threatened to embarrass national security bureaucracies, not information that threatened the national security of the United States. So secrecy is repeatedly used as a way for powerful bureaucracies to maintain control of discussion of these issues."

There is no real reason for the detail that he discusses in his book to be kept secret, he says. The details are now historic, and therefore the public and policy-makers can learn from them without risk. "Basic decisions of national security policy are made by a small handful of officials in Washington DC without the input of public debate. There is something fundamentally authoritarian and anti-democratic about the management of nuclear weapons. My book is an effort to restore some semblance of democracy to this system. This is information I think it's crucial for people to know."

"There can be an interesting debate about who is more qualified to determine what threatens the national interest – government officials, journalists, ordinary citizens – but I think each of us has to take personal responsibility for what he or she reveals, and I take that responsibility. I'm not going to reveal my sources and I tried really hard not to reveal anything that threatens the security of the United States – and I don't think I have."

Journalists, he believes, take a kind of Hippocratic oath both to "do no harm" and to protect their sources. "I think that there is an important role for mediators of information. I think it is irresponsible to release documents that could lead to people being harmed. I think some of the WikiLeaks things should have been more carefully scrutinised so that the names of people who work for the United States may not be put in physical jeopardy."

His reaction to Snowden's revelations is one of shock at the incompetence of the US government. "What's unfortunate is that the United States government is responsible for this problem – it has far too many secrets and far too many people with the security clearances able to access those secrets. One of the most significant things that has come out of the Snowden case to me is the revelation of how incompetent the government is at maintaining its own secrets."

"Again and again, what had been censored was information that threatened to embarrass national security bureaucracies, not information that threatened the national security of the United States"

Schlosser is concerned about the future of reporting. "I am a member of an endangered species unfortunately. There has never been a greater need for investigative journalism and yet there's a declining supply of it. I'm hoping that the transition from print to digital media will occur more quickly so that there are means of paying journalists through the delivery of digital media. What's horrible about what happened is that a small number of news aggregators have been able to get online first, and more cleverly get online, and pioneer a certain kind of parasitic news delivery: sites which don't pay journalists, which use the work of journalists that has been paid for by mainstream media organisations without paying →

→ the actual journalists. So we've created a feeling that news should be available for free. The notion that it should be available for free I think is insulting to the people that do it."

He doesn't want to discourage people from entering journalism because there is a wealth of subjects that need to be delved into, but compared with his first years in journalism, when The Atlantic supported him to go off diary and embark on long investigations, the likelihood of finding those opportunities as an unknown name are limited. "I encourage people who are going into journalism to really learn how to write but to also learn how to use a video camera and learn how to edit." ⊠

©Rachael Jolley
www.indexoncensorship.org

Rachael Jolley is editor of Index on Censorship

Portraits of a president

42(4): 103/106 | DOI: 10.1177/0306422013513391

South African President Jacob Zuma doesn't like the way artists depict him – and with an election in a few months' time, artists and the ANC are at loggersheads. **Natasha Joseph** reports

AT THE SOUTH African Broadcasting Corporation's offices during the apartheid era, censors had a special way of dealing with music the government didn't want heard. They hammered nails into LPs in an attempt to ensure that no DJ would be able to slip a banned or controversial disc on to the turntable and introduce listeners to dangerous ideas.

Music, art and films were routinely banned, with movies carefully watched by a board of censors determined to excise smut, blasphemy and inappropriate ideas about racial equality.

In 1962, the artist Ronald Harrison painted the banned African National Congress (ANC) leader Albert Luthuli as Jesus Christ. The painting, Black Christ, showed Luthuli crucified by Hendrik Verwoerd, prime minister of South Africa from 1958 to 1966 and the "architect of apartheid" in popular history. Verwoerd and John Vorster, minister of justice and Verwoerd's successor as prime minister from 1966, were depicted by Harrison as Roman soldiers. The painting offended Verwoerd's ultra-conservative government on three fronts. Not only was the ANC a banned organisation and Luthuli a banned person whose name and face had no place in the public domain, but this was a direct challenge to the then-entrenched

system of apartheid and "separate development". Worst of all, Harrison was seen as blaspheming for daring to portray Christ as a black man.

Harrison was arrested and the painting was banned. It was smuggled out of the country and into the United Kingdom – probably the only reason it wasn't destroyed. The painting remained in the UK until 1997: it now hangs in the South African National Gallery. Harrison died on 28 June 2011.

But these are old stories – they hark back to a time and a political system that is long gone.

Or do they?

In the past three years, South African art has been at the centre of a heated public debate around censorship, dignity and what's "appropriate" when it comes to depicting President Zuma.

Zuma does not enjoy a comfortable relationship with art or satire. In 2010, a year into his presidency, it was revealed that he was suing the Avusa Media group, the cartoonist Jonathan Shapiro – known by his pen name, Zapiro – and the former editor-in-chief of the country's biggest weekly newspaper, the Sunday Times, Mondli Makhanya, for a total of 5 million rands (about $501,086 million at the current exchange rate). Shapiro had drawn a →

ABOVE: Artist Ayanda Mabulu with his painting Umshini Wam, a depiction of Zuma, Cape Town, 28 August 2012

→ cartoon depicting Zuma unbuckling his trousers while his political allies held down a blindfolded and obviously traumatised Lady Justice. The cartoon, published in September 2008, was a reference to Zuma's acquittal on a rape charge in 2006. The cartoon was lambasted by the ANC as racist. In 2012, Zuma dropped the lawsuit.

But it's not just cartooning that gets the president's back up. His governing party is not a fan of more traditional portraiture either.

In May 2012 Charl Blignaut, an arts journalist working for the weekly newspaper City Press in Johannesburg, visited the Goodman Gallery, where an exhibition by the artist Brett Murray was being set up. Called Hail to the Thief, Murray's exhibition pulled no punches on the ANC – and one of the pieces, The Spear, depicted Zuma in the style of Victor Ivanov's poster, Lenin Lived, Lenin is Alive, Lenin Will Live. The president stood tall and proud, looking at a distant horizon – and was pictured with his genitals exposed. Blignaut wrote a review of the exhibition, and a fierce debate was held in the City Press newsroom about whether or not to publish the offending image. Eventually, it was featured – uncensored – in the paper's arts section. Four days later, a journalist from another newspaper contacted the ANC for its comment – and a storm erupted.

The ANC called for a boycott of City Press – the first time since the advent of democracy that any political party had done so. Copies of the newspaper were burned during a protest march in Durban. A church group called for Murray to be stoned to death. Towards the end of May 2012 the modern version of the censorship board, the Film and Publications Board, announced that it had sent a team to assess the painting for classification. Before it announced a 16N (no under 16s, contains nudity) rating, the painting was defaced by two men who walked in the Goodman Gallery and defaced

it with a large black painted "x". The Goodman Gallery appealed against the classification and won.

This was just the start though. Another artist, Ayanda Mabulu, has produced two paintings that have caused a massive outcry among supporters of the governing party, and particularly those loyal to Zuma. His first, 2010's Ngcono Ihlwempu Kunesibhanxo Sesityebi (translated from the original Zulu, that's Better Poor Than a Rich Puppet). Zuma was depicted in traditional African garb – and his genitals were exposed. The painting was ignored when it was first exhibited, but the furore around The Spear sparked a new interest – and extreme hostility towards Mabulu.

Most recently, Mabulu's Yakhal'inkomo – Black Man's Cry – became the hottest

As unhappiness with the ANC grows, and with national elections set for May 2014, it is likely that more artists, whether they're painters, cartoonists, sculptors, singers or writers, will register their displeasure

talking point of the 2013 Johannesburg Art Fair when the organisers asked him not to display it. The painting, which shows Zuma holding a police dog on a leash and standing on a prostrate man's head, was a comment on the Marikana massacre of 2012, in which 44 striking mineworkers were killed by police. Several artists, outraged by what they perceived as political interference and kowtowing to the government and sponsors, removed their work too. Eventually, Mabulu's painting was returned to the walls at the fair.

Lesley Perkes, who runs the public arts activist "disorganisation" artatwork, →

→ considered the possible consequences of political clampdowns on art in a piece published on the City Press opinion pages in October 2013:

"Arts, humanities and social services budgets are being decimated everywhere to make way for the far more important business of war and power.

"What better time for artists to make challenging work and for us to actively resist all attempts at censorship? If fear keeps us passive, we may as well move to North Korea. Worse, we may not need to move at all.

"Although the art fair denies being put under pressure from their partners, there is little doubt they made the decision because the pressure exists. It is invisible, often, and it is easy to deny. But it is pervasive...

"We do not need to resign ourselves to living in a world in which the bottom line is the only one, and badly drawn at that. We are alive."

It is clear that there is a war brewing between the ANC and artists – particularly worrying in light of the country's history of sometimes violent censorship. As unhappiness with the ANC grows – and with national elections set for May 2014 – it is likely that more artists, whether they're painters, cartoonists, sculptors, singers or writers, will register their displeasure. And there's a real risk that the government will use not just its political muscle but its monetary might – hitting artists where it hurts, through funding cuts. ☒

© Natasha Joseph
www.indexoncensorship.org

Natasha Joseph is a journalist based in South Africa

Stamping on the moderates

42(4): 107/109 | DOI: 10.1177/0306422013513103

The Chinese authorities are cracking down hard on the popular New Citizens' Movement, even though, as **Xiao Shu** argues, its leaders are only trying to protect rights already guaranteed under the constitution

WHEN LAWYER SUI Muqing announced through his Sina Weibo account that he planned to take to the streets with a placard to protest against the treatment of one of his clients, web users in China rallied behind him and the story became a trending topic on the micro-blogging website.

The Guangzhou lawyer was moved to protest against police, who had violated the rights of his client, detained dissident Guo Feixiong, and refused to allow him access to a lawyer.

State police secretly detained Guo on 8 August 2013 for his activism and especially because of his support for southern China's New Citizens' Movement.

His crime, they said, was disturbing public order. Despite a legal requirement to contact his family within 24 hours, the police did not do so until 17 August. And although there are no restrictions on access to a lawyer for those arrested for ordinary offences such as disturbing public order, the police continue to refuse to allow Sui to see his client.

After five failed attempts to see Guo and a court's refusal to allow him to bring a case against the police, Sui, having exhausted legal channels, found himself with no option but to risk arrest by announcing plans for a public protest on 6 October.

This case is just one small part of the tragic and drawn-out suppression of the New Citizens' Movement. More than 30 members of the movement have been detained since the crackdown began in March this year. The detainees include initiator of the movement, Xu Zhiyong, and Wang Gongquan, well known in China as the founder of private equity firm CDH Investments. The scale and severity of the attacks on these people far outstrip those taken against participants in the Charter 08 movement. Back then only Liu Xiaobo was arrested.

The Chinese government clearly regards the New Citizens' Movement as a major threat that needs to be struck hard regardless of any damage caused to the image of the new administration.

The question is why, when the New Citizens' Movement is in fact entirely moderate. It aims to do nothing more than win for the people those rights already guaranteed in the constitution. For the movement's supporters, China's biggest political challenge is that, without those rights, there is no way to constrain authority, which therefore stands unopposed and without regard →

ABOVE: Protester wears a mask depicting Xu Zhiyong, founder of the New Citizens' Movement, Chinese National Day

Credit: PH Yang/Demotix/Press Association Images

→ for law or morality. Those rights must be won if civil society is to strengthen and there is to be reform and peaceful change in the country.

The measured and peaceful approach of the New Citizens' Movement sits well with the public, and this has allowed it to grow. Its mealtime gatherings were already attracting thousands at the start of the year. Its campaign on equality in education received support from tens of thousands of students and parents. The movement repre-

sents a breakthrough for China's civil society, not just because of its size, but more importantly because it has reached the mainstream and earned backing from many prominent figures. The debate it sparked on equality in education forced the Ministry of Education to change the rules so the teenage children of migrant workers no longer had to travel back to their home villages to take the university entrance examination. Such change is a rare event indeed.

The New Citizens' Movement's strategy is to focus on rights as a solution to practical issues, all within a framework of democracy and the rule of law, to encourage greater public participation and align with mainstream society and opinion. The strategy has proved successful, and that success has brought disaster.

If the authorities did not regard constitutional government as a foe, if they accepted the constitution as the consensus of both government and the people and were willing to move towards its implementation, then, even if they did not welcome the New Citizens' Movement's success, at least they might tolerate it. For the aims of the movement are to advance the constitution: Wang Gongquan, one of its founders, described what the movement was doing as "constructive opposition".

But the authorities have decided against tolerance. In March those opposed to the constitution rose up and their attacks became stronger and were given the status of a "public opinion struggle", a propaganda war for ideological dominance. The hardliners could not ignore the sudden growth of the New Citizens' Movement, which they inevitably regarded as an "enemy of the state". So alongside taking action against the intellectuals and the internet, they also moved decisively against the New Citizens' Movement. Arrest warrants were issued and one by one advocates of the movement, Guo Feixiong, Xu Zhiyong and Wang Gongquan, landed in jail.

This is a disaster not just for the movement, but for the nation. It sets us in China more firmly on a path away from constitutional government and a modern society. And Guo Feixiong's experiences may be the bloodiest of the whole affair. He has been tortured in prison in the past, and we cannot be sure he has not been tortured in prison again, which may be why the police are so determined to keep him from his lawyer.

What will his fate be? What will the fate of Xu and Wang and all the detainees be? The answers will show us which direction China is to take. ☒

Translated by Roddy Flagg
©Xiao Shu
www.indexoncensorship.org

Xiao Shu is a former Southern Weekly columnist and is active in the New Citizens' Movement. In February 2013, he was among a group of public figures that called for the Chinese government to ratify the International Covenant on Civil and Political Rights. He was temporarily put under house arrest in August after being forcibly returned to Guangzhou from Beijing

Gambia gagged?

42(4): 110/112 | DOI: 10.1177/0306422013513859

Gambia has a new journalism school but it is still one of the most dangerous places in west Africa for journalists to work. **Buya Jammeh** reports on the country's ongoing battle for free expression

IN GAMBIA, WHERE there is a great deal of political uncertainty and free expression is constantly undermined by a volatile environment, it is often journalists and political opponents that are the most most vulnerable.

Following the July 1994 military coup on the 22 July 1994 that ended the 30-year rule of Gambia's immediate post-independence leader Sir Dawda Jawara's 30 years of democratic rule, many Gambians were confident that the tiny west African nation has would develop a thriving democracy unencumbered by corruption and cronyism.

But 19 years later such hopes are all but dead. Coup leader Yahya Jammeh is still in power, the president of a government notorious for violations of human rights. His regime has a shameful record of arbitrary arrests, suppression of the press, and intimidation of journalists.

This autumn a group of Gambian human rights activists led by Amadou Scattred Janneh, a former information minister who was sentenced to life imprisonment by the Jammeh regime, held a protest at the Ritz Carlton Hotel in New York where Jammeh was staying while attending the United Nations General Assembly. The protesters called on Jammeh to answer for human rights violations in Gambia, particularly those relating to journalists.

Three days after the demonstration, a prominent member of Jammeh's ruling party, the MP Pa Malick Ceesay, sent a message to Omar Bah, editor of the US-based Gambian dissident online newspaper American Street News (ASN), threatening to harm his parents, who live in Gambia.

Gambian journalists have fought hard for freedom of expression. And there has been some good news in the past 12 months. In March the first journalism training institute in nearly half a century of independence came into being when the Gambia National Training Authority accredited the Gambia Press Union's pioneering journalism school, set up with help from the Danish International Development Agency. The Gambia Press Union called the accreditation of the centre an "unprecedented development in a country that has never had a formal structure for journalism education," according to Panapress.

The European input was welcomed by Gambian journalists – but it has not been without strings. In January 2013, the European Union demanded that the Jammeh regime repeal authoritarian media laws, give foreign diplomats access to prisons and abolish the death penalty.

There can be no doubt that the Gambian regime's attitude to freedom of expression is draconian. In April, Jammeh's government got the Public Utilities Regulatory Authority to ban the use of free internet phone services using voice over internet protocol (VoIP).

ABOVE: Gambian President Yahya Jammeh addresses the 68th United Nations General Assembly at UN headquarters in New York

The government warned that anyone using VoIP phone services was depriving the country of revenue from international and national calls – and was therefore committing an economic crime. It subsequently stepped back from the ban, but still imposed a stiff charge on internet cafes to register for use of VoIP.

Worse, however, was to come. In July the government pushed through legislation imposing sanctions on government officials and other individuals who gives stories →

→ to Gambian online news outlets outside the country – with a penalty of a 15-year jail term or a fine of more than £50,000 (US$ 79,695) for miscreants.

Fatou Camara, a former press officer for the president and prominent popular television presenter, was arrested in September and detained by the Gambian National Intelligence Agency for more than 72 hours without charge. She was subsequently held in prison for the best part of a month but has now managed to leave the country.

According to American Street News, Fatou's arrest and detention was the result of her involvement with the Senegalese musician Youssou N'dour's Television Future Media, a Senegal-based TV station that often reports critically on the Gambian dictatorship.

Leigh's arrest was linked to his criticisms of the regime's execution of nine prisoners by firing squad in August 2012, which caused international outrage. The killings were condemned by the African Commission on Human and People's Rights, the European Union, Amnesty International and the Senegalese government. Leigh was released from custody in May after protests from European and African governments and human rights organisations.

There are no signs of improvement on the horizon if further pressure is not applied externally. Meanwhile Gambian journalists struggle against all odds to make their voices heard. ☒

©Buya Jammeh
www.indexoncensorship.org

Yahya Jammeh's regime has a shameful record of arbitrary arrests and intimidation of journalists

Also, in July, Freedom House condemned amendments to Gambia's Information and Communications Act – passed by the National Assembly – which penalises those who spread "false news or information" against the government. These amendments further restrict freedom of expression, press freedom and internet freedom in Gambia and demonstrate the government's open hostility towards the media.

Another stain on Jammeh's record is religious tolerance. In August 2012, a prominent Islamic scholar and imam, BaKawusu Fofana, abruptly fled the country and sought refuge in Casamance in southern Senegal after being detained for nine days, and, he says, tortured. In December that year, another outspoken imam, Baba Leigh, was seized by Gambian authorities.

Buya Jammeh is a Gambian journalist. He tweets @jammehb

China's darkest corner

42(4): 113/118 | DOI: 10.1177/0306422013512962

Campaigner **Alim Seytoff** looks at the suppression of the Muslim Uighur people in China over the decades and speaks to activists about their experiences

IT HAS BEEN a bloody year for the Uighur people of China. Throughout 2013, restrictions around religious practice have been tightened, land belonging to Uighur people has been illegally seized and the authorities in the region have deployed heavy-handed policing tactics. State-sponsored violence has led, unsurprisingly, to the escalation of tensions. In the Chinese government's 64-year administration of the region, 2013 has been one of the worst in history, particularly since Xi Jinping assumed the presidency of the People's Republic of China in March this year. Serious incidents across the region, in Yilkiqi, Akyol, Hanerik, Lukqun and Maralbeshi, have highlighted not only the Chinese state's failure genuinely to address legitimate Uighur grievances, but also its willingness to sanction security officials' increasing use of lethal force against Uighur civilians. The Chinese government's aggressive policies of cultural repression, targeting Uighur identity, language, culture religious beliefs and practices, has left China's Uighurs feeling constantly under threat.

In recent months, there have been hundreds of arrests, and police and members of the security forces have shot and killed dozens of Uighurs during protests and riots. Police and security officials have also lost their lives. In Lukqun on 26 June,

16 Uighur protesters and two police officers were among the dead; on 11 October, security personnel killed at least five Uighurs in Yingwusitang township in Yarkand county near Kashgar. Throughout the summer, Uighurs were detained on charges of religious extremism and distribution of material, deemed a threat to national stability.

The tight constraints placed on religious practice are widespread. Religious leaders such as imams are required to attend political education classes to ensure compliance with Chinese Communist Party (CCP) regulations and policies; only state-approved versions of the Quran and sermons are permitted, with all unapproved religious texts treated as "illegal" publications liable to confiscation, with criminal charges levied against those in possession of them. Outward expressions of faith, such as men wearing beards or women wearing headscarves, are forbidden in government workplaces, hospitals and some private businesses.

State employees cannot enter a mosque, and neither can any individual under the age of 18 – a measure not in force in the rest of China. Organised private religious education is proscribed and facilitators of private classes about Islam are frequently charged with conducting "illegal" religious activities; students, teachers and government →

XINJIANG

HOME TO CHINA'S UIGHUR POPULATION

→ workers are prohibited from fasting during Ramadan. Uighurs are not permitted to undertake Hajj, unless it is with an expensive official tour, in which state officials carefully vet applicants.

During a recent visit to Turkey to discuss the ongoing tensions, one Uighur activist remarked, "There are three choices for the Uighur people now in China: accept Chinese cultural assimilation, go to prison for refusing to accept it, or die resisting it." I asked him what option he would choose. He defiantly said: "None!" I asked what he really meant. He said, "I am not Han and don't want to be Han. Uighurs are Uighurs and Han are Han. We are simply two completely different kinds of peoples with different languages, cultures, identity, religious beliefs, traditions and values. I am Uighur and my ancestors are Uighur. I don't mind learning and speaking the Chinese language but I simply cannot accept cultural assimilation. I want to speak my beautiful Uighur language, practise my own religion, live within my own culture and tradition without state

encroachment. I certainly don't want to go to prison. It looks like I'll go to prison eventually for asserting my identity and for not accepting cultural assimilation. But I am not going to outright resist the Chinese government because I will most likely be killed as a 'violent terrorist' by Chinese security forces for my non-violent expression of resistance."

The message sent by the Chinese authorities to the Uighur people is loud and clear: resisting assimilation is futile. The end of Uighur identity is in sight, whether or not this is voluntarily accepted. The Chinese government will use any means necessary to achieve their aims, using lethal force to deal with any kind of dispute or confrontation. Those involved in these confrontations will continue to be blamed and labelled "violent terrorists". International media and observers will continue not to be told the truth and prevented from giving an accurate account of what is going on. Chinese officials will simply cover up the killings and deny they have taken place. The story will be spun to both the domestic and international media in a way that serves the best interests of the Chinese government. No Uighur person, the Chinese Communist Party seems to be saying, can change what is inevitable.

"Is this inevitable?" I asked the activist in Turkey. He said, "No. This is the 21st century. This is a digital century. Yes, we live in fear and we are being punished for being who we are on a daily basis, but when the right time comes, we can tell the truth to the whole world in an instant." He added that in an age of globalisation, cultural and ethnic genocides cannot take place without the world knowing, no matter how much power a country wields.

He said: "We have survived many invasions, occupations and massacres in our history, and we will surely survive this cultural genocide."

Stifling dissent

The recent crackdown on Uighurs began following unrest in the Xinjiang (known as East Turkestan to Uighurs) capital Urumqi in July 2009, when a series of security policies were implemented, including the use of violence against ordinary Uighur citizens. On 5 July 2009, thousands of Uighurs assembled peacefully in Urumqi's People's Square to protest against the state's failure to uphold their human, political and social rights. Chinese authorities indiscriminately fired on demonstrators, sparking days of unrest and resulting in the deaths of hundreds of people. To this day, Chinese officials fail to give a clear explanation of what happened: more than 130,000 troops were deployed to the region, including soldiers from other regions of China, in a bid to restore order and crack down on Uighur protesters. These actions effectively turned the region into a police state. Officials laid the blame squarely on the Uighur population, stating that it had evidence that many involved in the unrest had received training from al Qaeda-affliated insurgents. Since then, the government has specifically targeted Uighurs' freedom of expression, freedom of speech and freedom of religion in the name of security. In the immediate aftermath of the massacre, authorities initiated an unprecedented information blackout in the region for nearly a year, blocking both the internet and international telephone communications. Hundreds of Uighur websites were shut down. Prominent Uighur activists, bloggers and journalists were arrested and given long prison sentences. Uighurs who had uploaded images and video footage of Chinese security forces attacking protesters on 5 July were arrested and dozens of people are still missing. Uig-

Accusations of terrorism and the use of brutal force are consistently used as tools to silence legitimate Uighur dissent

hurs who had communicated with one another for religious purposes, or watched and downloaded religious content online, were severely punished.

To the 10.2 million Uighurs living there, the region is known as East Turkestan, referring to both the campaign for autonomy and the Turkic origins of the Uighur people. The Uighur struggle for autonomy dates back to 1949, when the Chinese military forcibly invaded East Turkestan, and in 1955 it was renamed Xinjiang, which translates as "new territory". The Xinjiang Uighur Autonomous Region was created, and the government promised Uighurs they would be entitled to self-rule and that the language, traditions and culture of the Uighur people would be protected. But this was never the case, and by the late 1960s, those working to protect Uighur heritage and secure a more promising future for their people were branded as "counter-revolutionaries". Many of them were imprisoned. Though it is →

→ not known how many people have been killed, imprisoned and tortured since 1949, some sources have estimated somewhere in the region of one million people. The Uighur language is banned from schools and universities. And since the 11 September 2001 terrorist attack on the United States, China has waged its own "war on terror", using the fact that the Uighur population are practising Muslims to justify its brutal clampdown.

When Xi Jinping assumed the presidency of the Communist Party he became the fifth generation of Chinese leaders to rule the region, and it was hoped that things would change. He was presented with a once-in-a-decade opportunity to genuinely embrace political reform. Instead, the newly appointed leader has offered little hope for those yearning for China to begin a transition to democracy and embrace universal human rights.

There are no official reports of how many Uighurs have been killed in recent months. Security in the region remains tight and arrests of Uighur people continue. Independent observers have access to very little information apart from scant accounts provided by the Chinese authorities and promoted through the official media. None of these accounts have been verified by external or objective sources. According to reports published by the New York Times and Radio Free Asia, the Chinese state has not revealed the full truth about events.

In a June 2013 clash between the authorities and protesters in Hanerik township near Hotan in the south of the region, official news source Tianshan Net reported that no one had died as a result of the clashes. Yet Radio Free Asia, citing local officials, reported that security forces had fired on demonstrating Uighurs rather than responding with restraint to civilian violence. Quoting local residents, a New York Times article reported that "scores of young men" were killed in the incident. Communications

between those at the demonstration and the outside world were cut in an attempt to control the spread of information so it is hard to verify the truth.

In the only state media reference to an August 2013 incident in Yilkiqi, the Kashgar Daily reported on the heroism of a member of the security forces who was allegedly killed during a clash with so-called terrorists. By contrast, Radio Free Asia reported that 22 Uighurs were gunned down while at prayer. According to local sources, the bodies of the dead were buried in a mass grave in order to cover up the killings. In Maralbeshi, Radio Free Asia reported the deaths of 21 people, while in Lukqun some reports say the death toll was as high as 46, a number unreported in the Chinese media. There were also conflicting reports concerning an incident in Akyol, where three people were said to have been killed when security forces fired on protesters.

On 8 October 2013, both the Chinese and international media, including the BBC, reported that 256 people were under investigation for "spreading destabilising rumours" online. A further 139 people were investigated for spreading rumours about "jihad or Muslim holy war or other religious ideas". Tianshan Net reported that 110 people had been detained; 94 of them were arrested on administrative charges and 16 on criminal ones. In addition, 164 individuals were given warnings. Without offering any details, the Chinese authorities labelled those in detention as "extremists", closing down any debate about the truth of Uighur claims. Though many incidents are isolated, it appears the authorities have adopted a policy of using heavy-handed tactics to suppress any protest often sparked off by local grievances. Accusations of terrorism and the use of brutal force are consistently used as tools to silence legitimate Uighur dissent.

There has been very little economic growth in the region, despite initiatives set out in

May 2010's Xinjiang Work Forum, which aimed to boost the economy through state investment as well as providing jobs and improving education. The forum was initially prompted by Chinese officials' tacit acknowledgment that policies in the region had failed to bring about economic and social development on par with growth in other parts of the country.

Inequalities stemming from the failure of previous policies, the effects of which have been felt largely by the region's Uighur and other non-Han populations, were undeniably a factor in the turbulent unrest of July 2009. However, the policies set out at the forum failed to address inequalities and discrimination, giving rise to further tensions.

Four years after the turmoil in Urumqi, the region's development strategy remains devoid of an adequate framework for evaluating and improving the harsh economic conditions the non-Han community experiences, including unequal income distribution, high levels of poverty, forced migration and continued appropriation of Uighur land for state development initiatives. The forum meets annually and is attended by top-level officials, but is marked by the absence of any Uighur representation. At its core, regional development is plagued by the lack of consultation with, and participation by, Uighurs and other non-Han residents. This means those who are directly affected by these policies have absolutely no say in their implementation.

Though I concur with what the Uighur activist expressed in Turkey, I have often felt terribly sorry for Chinese President Xi Jinping and members of the country's Politbureau. They have the mindset of 19th century Chinese mandarins. Why else do they resort to 19th century policies when it comes to dealing with different cultures and beliefs? If these leaders thought like 21st century politicians, they would start genuinely embracing political reform. They would begin the transition to democracy by embracing universal human rights and finding a peaceful resolution to the "Uighur Question". ☒

©Alim Seytoff
www.indexoncensorship.org

Alim Seytoff is general secretary of the Uyghur American Society

III

2013: A year of clashes and turmoil

7 March: Four people are killed and eight injured in a knife attack in Korla, South of the capital Urumqi. One person was arrested, but the ethnicity of the suspect or victims could not be confirmed [check link]

23 April: 21 people are killed, including 15 police officers and officials. The foreign ministry said it had been a planned attack by a "violent terrorist group", but ethnic groups questioned this

20 May: Seven Han Chinese workers are killed in an attack at a dam construction site. Hundreds of Uighurs are detained for questioning

26 June: 35 people are killed in clashes as rioters attack police stations and set fire to police cars in Lukqun. Sixteen of those killed by the rioters are Uighurs. Two police officers are also killed

26 June-31 August: Across Xinjiang, 139 people are detained and 164 people given warnings after being accused of religious extremism and distribution of material that threatened stability

28 June: State-run media report more than 100 people on motorbikes, some wielding knives, attack a police station

28 June: A 30-year-old Uyghuir man was killed in Uchturpan after he allegedly stabbed two people, including a police officer, because he refused to shave his beard whilst officials conducted street patrol aimed at curbing religious attire

28 June: After shouting religious slogans as they leave midday prayers, two Uighurs are shot dead by police and one is injured

11 July-9 October: Police report that video and audio files "spreading religious extremism" have been viewed over 5,100 times and downloaded 1,201 times. The files are said to have been uploaded by a 17-year-old student from Jiashi county

7 August: at least three Uighurs are killed and more than 50 left injured, including a four-year-old girl, after clashes in No 16 Village of Aykol town in Aksu. Between 300 and 400 people are detained

13 August: Two Uighur men are sentenced to death and three more are jailed over the 23 April clashes

20 August: At least 16 Uighurs accused of terrorism and illegal religious activity are shot dead by Chinese authorities in the Yilkiqi township in Kargilik

23 August: Up to 12 Uighurs are shot dead and 20 others wounded in a raid on what the authorities referred to as a "terrorist" facility in Poskam county

9 September: Following an argument, a Uighur fruitseller in his 20s is shot and seriously wounded by police

13 September: Three people are sentenced to death and one person sentenced to 25 years in jail over the clashes in Lukqun in June

18 September: Authorities place a Chinese flag at the head of a mosque in the Aksu area, forcing Uighurs to bow to it when they worship

24 September: About 100 Uighurs are rounded up after fleeing Yunnan and heading towards Lao. Women and children are among the detainees. On the same day, eight Uighurs are arrested by Yunnan police in Mohan and transferred to Xinjiang police

28 September: After police fire on a group of Uighurs at Yarkland railway station, one man is killed

1 October: Nine Uighurs are detained after marching to the Yarkand county government offices to protest against the 28 September attacks

3 October: Police shoot and kill two Uighurs in a private residence located in Abu Dona Village No 16

11 October: Five Uighurs are shot dead by security forces in Yingwusitang township in Yarkand county

Sources: al Jazeera, BBC, China Daily, Dawn, Radio Free Asia

Should young people be able to scrub away embarrassing social media posts?

HEAD TO HEAD: Alice Kirkland & Pam Cowburn

42(4): 119/121 | DOI: 10.1177/0306422013513413

Dear Alice,

Having grown up in the olden days when there were no smart phones and no social media and the internet was referred to as the "information superhighway", there is little public evidence of my misspent youth. This, frankly, is the only good thing about being 40. Any incriminating photos (taken by an actual camera, developed at the chemist's and then carefully sorted in case your mum went through them) are languishing in shoe boxes in my friends' attics. Unless I suddenly become famous, of course.

There are diaries, letters and scrapbooks that it would pain me to read locked in a room on my own. The thought of anyone else seeing them is too awful to contemplate but – embarrassment aside – could there be consequences for my career if these were to see the light of day? (Some of those perms were really bad.)

Enshrining the "right to be forgotten" in law would have drastic consequences for freedom of expression. Such a right would be open to abuse by politicians and others who wish to manipulate the past for their own gain. It's fair enough that adults should have to live with the consequences of their own actions.

Now that I have two kids I wonder should we apply the same rules to young people who aren't old enough to know better? Maybe legislation, like the new Californian law that will allow young people under 18 the right to scrub embarrassing content or information that they have posted, could protect children from having to live with the embarrassment, not to mention the more serious consequences, of their youthful mistakes for the rest of their lives.

Best wishes,
Pam

Dear Pam,

I understand why, as a parent, you may have concerns about the implications for your children of what they post on social →

Credit: Mark Boardman/www.markboardman.com

media sites. However, having grown up in the first generation to use such websites I feel there is an over-emphasised, and sometimes sensationalised, view in the media that young people are going to come to harm.

I completely understand that there will always be people who will manipulate the system and attempt to use it in harmful manner. But just as your and my generation were taught not to get into cars with strangers, so young people today are taught not to interact with strangers online.

There is no need for a "right to be forgotten". I am 23 years old. I started using social media when I was 11 or 12. It has been a part of my life since then. I grew up understanding that there would be consequences from what I posted online. Admittedly, there was no way imaginable that I could have conceived how much of a giant social media is today. But even my 12-year-old self, obsessed with MySpace, Bebo and MSN Messenger, knew not to post something online that could be harmful to me, or others.

If I knew 10 years ago how to use social media, surely children today have an even better understanding of what to post online than I ever did.

All the best,
Alice

Dear Alice,

As anyone who has witnessed a two-year-old work their way around an iPhone knows, children today have a symbiotic relationship with technology. Photographs are no longer taken on special occasions but on a daily basis by a phone not a camera – sometimes wielded by a five-year-old who already knows how to text the images to Granny. Teaching children about the impact of sharing their images and thoughts should start in primary school – and, given the propensity of doting parents to share news of their offspring's every bowel movement, perhaps training should be included in antenatal classes as well.

And will children really care about protecting their futures? I was a vehement anti-smoker at 10 but saving my dinner money to buy packets of 10 Regal King Size at 14, because, despite all the health warnings from school and my parents, my teenage self could not conceive that my actions might have an impact on my future. And if I didn't care about my health, why would I care about something as unimportant as my career?

All the best,
Pam

Dear Pam,

I agree that the use of social media should be taught to young children. I learnt how to use social media from my peers, and as I got older my school and university both encouraged me to use social media and warned me of the dangers of it.

However, these days, for every job interview I go to, I'm expected to make sure my Facebook page is private and that my Twitter account only says positive things. Can I ask you whether before you went for your first job interview you went through your personal diary and ripped out pages containing something you wouldn't wish your would-be employer to read? I hope it doesn't sound too harsh to say that I didn't think so.

For the majority of people today social media is their diary. How is it fair that young people have to self-censor their diaries before attending a job interview or fear that clients might read what they get up to? At least social media shows that we have a life – though it's most likely to be pretty mundane and just like everyone else's.

Surely enough background checks are made on people already? Criminal records and references from past employers are the norm for any job position. Do these checks alone not offer enough of an insight into a would-be employee? Then there are the face-to-face interviews. Speaking to someone in an interview must offer much more of an insight into their personality than trawling through page after page of a Facebook feed.

All the same, I have heard on numerous occasions that employers are more likely to employ someone with an open Facebook page than one that is private. A private Facebook page suggests the user has something to hide.

Best wishes,
Alice

Dear Alice,

The Crown Prosecution Service says that youth should be taken into account when deciding whether to prosecute over offensive social media posts. I think employers should also apply a similar approach. But until those recruiting have grown up with social media themselves, will they be so understanding? A boozy snapshot is one thing but what about comments that are deemed to be unacceptable? Earlier this year, Paris Brown, the 17-year-old youth crime commissioner for Kent, was forced to resign because of racist, homophobic and offensive tweets she had posted between the ages of 14 and 16. Most young people won't have the Mail on Sunday scouring their Twitter feed – but who knows when their past will be looked into, and what the consequences of that will be?

All the best,
Pam

Dear Pam,

I think employers should understand how much social media matters to people today and take that into account when making decisions about hiring.

You mentioned earlier the California law that from 2015 will allow minors to request that social media and websites eliminate content. I will not be the only person who wonders whether, if there is an option to have all content removed, young people will actually be more inclined to post content they may later regret. A law like this is an invitation to young people to act inappropriately.

And there is always the delete button. I can't quite get my head around the fact that a new law needs to be brought in when there is a simple button that does the same thing. Yes, the picture, post, link or comment that you have just deleted is still out there somewhere in cyberspace; yes, that picture, post, link or comment is now the property of the social media site you shared it with (you'd know this if you read the small print, but no one does). But the likelihood of anyone retrieving one tiny, insignificant picture from the billions out there is minuscule. Why introduce a law that will only encourage young people to upload inappropriate content knowing full well that they can request to have it taken down again when it suits them, when they are applying for university or a job?

The whole point of history, to me, is to learn from it and how can it be learnt from if it is has been erased? What if people started deleting parts of their personal history, is that right? Foreign Secretary William Hague gave a big political speech when he was 16. People do important things before they are 18. They shouldn't edit them out of history.

Best wishes,
Alice ☒

www.indexoncensorship.org

Alice Kirkland, 23, is a recent graduate of Liverpool John Moores University
Pam Cowburn, 40, is a less recent graduate of Glasgow University, and has two children

Using cyber-bullying to target dissent

42(4): 122/124 | DOI: 10.1177/0306422013512242

Attacked by the government and the populist press alike, political bloggers and Twitter users in Greece struggle to make their voices heard, argues **Christos Syllas**

WITHOUT A DOUBT, the suppression of online free speech has become an increasingly important piece of Greece's political puzzle. It forms part of the wider landscape of human rights violations, xenophobic and racist attacks and decreased rights for workers. The attack on online media has meant widespread censorship of the facts, in effect the news, which makes a true representation of the current political conflict impossible. When trying to report the news that mainstream media chooses to ignore, activists, alternative media and prominent bloggers have long experienced serious levels of censorship. And now it's getting worse.

In recent years, much of the mainstream media's reporting has been closely aligned with the government's agenda. This is nothing new. The government has often applied pressure to types of reporting it doesn't like, even pulling the plug on Athens's Indymedia website, established in 2001 by anti-authoritarian campaigners and radical leftists on 11 April 2011.

Indymedia had often reported on cases of police brutality and exposed the relationship between the neo-Nazi party Golden Dawn and some members of the police. At the time, Adonis Georgiadis, an MP for ruling party New Democracy (ND) and known for his hatred of Indymedia's editorial stance, sent a tweet to Public Order Minister Nikos Dendias, congratulating him for taking down Indymedia. In the end, after a series of protests and rallies in support of the outlet, it managed to keep going.

Prominent bloggers and social media users have also been targeted for their public writing and comments as well as for their investigative reports. An example that best illustrates the intense political bullying coming from the government is the case of the blogger Gerogriniaris, which, translated into English, means "grumpy old man".

Gerogriniaris successfully exposed the role of Truth Team, a group that first emerged prior to the national elections of 2012, with a mission support New Democracy (ND),

ABOVE: Riot police at a demonstration to voice outrage over the murder of hip hop activist Pavlos Fyssas, 20 September 2013

the current party of government. Although the team denied expressing ND's official views, it has turned out to be a propaganda machine designed to attack anyone who opposes the ruling party's views. Opposition party supporters, in particular the Coalition of the Radical Left, (SYRIZA), frequently face attacks, but the group also targets leftists, anarchists and anyone with a "communist orientation".

Gerogriniaris's investigations found that Truth Team, which closely monitors television, internet, radio and the printed press, regularly distorts statements and fabricates stories and facts, according to reports from magazine Unfollow.

George Mouroutis, head of the press office of the General Secretariat of the Prime Minister, and in charge of the Truth Team, has

For many, anonymous activism is still the safest way

been at the epicentre of this case. He often throws out unsubstantiated accusations and threats on Twitter. →

→ Gerogriniaris, who has been on the receiving end of these threats, offers some explanation. In an interview on 1 October, he told me, "I am not a journalist, I don't belong to any party. All I am trying to do is to check if the government speaks the truth. Since I reported on Truth Team I have been publicly getting a lot of threats of prosecution from Mouroutis." He adds that, although he has been bullied and threatened a number of times by Golden Dawn members, he is "more impressed by the constant and methodical pattern of those who confront me when it comes to New Democracy issues. I believe that those in power hold a crypto-fascist mentality – a very dangerous one."

Gerogriniaris has got used to trolling and bullying from several accounts that support ND's interests. When he writes something, he prefers to have strong arguments in order to defend himself.

Many bloggers, activists and ordinary people use Twitter and other sites as vehicles to engage in political struggle, and many of them choose to be anonymous for their own safety. Many of them are known out on the streets and participate in protests.

"GP", a member of an anti-Nazi group in Athens that organises anti-fascist rallies and raises awareness on immigrants and refugee issues, is quite confident about the anonymity status on social media. Having received several threatening emails and direct messages on Twitter, GP believes that anonymous activism is still the safest way. "If I was not so afraid about my life, I would go on with my real name," he says. He has received fake pictures of anti-fascists being hung, and threats such as "we know who you are, we are looking for you". So far, he adds, "I've managed to cope with any kind of threat or bullying." When asked about the ways in which a threat can be carried out, he says, "Sometimes, you get followed by accounts with little influence. They usually do not engage in political conversations. They seem very neutral. They only post songs, movie trailers etc. When something big enters the agenda and I state my opinion, I get reactive and inflammatory comments. Just like that, out of the blue. There's a lot of monitoring on social media I guess. I remember once, I was tweeting during a pro-immigrant rally, and I was bullied by a Nazi group in the Netherlands…"

Those who voice alternative opinions continue to face threats from far-right media, whether it be online and or in print. And, increasingly, intimidation tactics are used not only by radical groups, but also by the current regime. For individuals that dare to challenge the current political environment, the war has just begun. ☒

©Christos Syllas
www.indexoncensorship.org

Christos Syllas is a freelance journalist, based in Athens, Greece

Family values?

42(4): 125/127 | DOI: 10.1177/0306422013513525

When the editor of popular Indian newspaper The Hindu was pushed out after two years, commentators asked whether this signalled a move to turn the clock back and make the newspaper a family-run affair once more, writes **Eklavya Gupte**

WHEN SIDDHARTH VARADARAJAN was appointed as the editor-in-chief of popular Indian national newspaper The Hindu two years ago, it was taken as a signal of a change of pace and attitude. It was expected to signal a move away from the old days of the family-run enterprise towards a business-like future where an experienced editor would make editorial decisions based on journalistic values. Two years later, Varadarajan is no longer the editor-in-chief, and all the indications are that this is a backwards-move.

In late October, Varadarajan was ousted from his post. This took place after the old guard at publisher Kasturi and Sons Ltd voted to overhaul the management of the newspaper. The move was spearheaded by its chairman Narasimhan Ram, who used his casting vote to carry the day. Varadarajan, who was re-designated as contributing editor and senior columnist, resigned after the announcement.

This is a troubling and unfortunate precedent in a country where so many institutions, ranging from private enterprises and companies like Reliance and Tata to the Congress Party, are largely still centred on or run by a single family. And the media is no exception. Other media families include the Sahu Jain family, who own the Times Group and its parent company, Bennett, Coleman & Co Ltd, which publishes the Times of India, the biggest selling English newspaper in India and indeed the world. With The Hindu being a reputed newspaper and publishing house, it begs the question, will it again be a professionally run news publication or does the Kasturi family, its members and their interests still hold sway?

Unfortunately, it seems the latter maybe true. Varadarajan was the first editor in The Hindu's 135-year history to be appointed from outside the Kasturi clan, and this tenure has only lasted two years. The Hindu is viewed in India as less populist than many other national newspapers, a serious publication dedicated to thoughtful reportage and investigative journalism with a left-of-centre slant. This is very much needed in a country where the news media continues to be dominated by the brash and brazen Times of India, infamous for its puff pieces or advertorials, along with an army of chest-thumping and jingoistic 24-hour news channels.

It is likely that The Hindu will continue in its sober vein but the removal of Varadarajan does not seem to be a step in the right →

ABOVE: A shop in Alappuzha, Kerala advertises The Hindu, viewed as one of India's less populist newspapers. In its 135-year history, it has only enjoyed two years of editorial management from someone outside the Kasturi family clan

→ direction. Initial signs do not look very promising.

The 48-year-old editor had made an immediate impact, making The Hindu a more readable and tougher newspaper, with a penchant for hard-hitting investigative journalism. It is one of the only Indian newspapers that has a correspondent based in Africa, appointed during-Varadarajan's two years in charge. It was also one of the very few national papers that included a vast amount of reportage and stories on the Maoist insurgencies taking place in eastern and central India.

As a backdrop to this drama, it is important to remember that next year India will be holding its first general elections in five years. Narendra Modi, who is the opposition Bharatiya Janata Party's candidate for Prime Minister, looks set to win. But Modi is one of the most polarising figures in India at the moment, infamous for his alleged role in the Gujarat Hindu-Muslim riots of 2002. Since then he has been elected as the Chief Minister of Gujarat for three elections in a row and is now expected to be the next leader of India.

One statement in particular showed how divisive Modi is even at The Hindu. A couple of days after Varadarajan's resignation, Narasimhan Ravi, the newspaper's new editor-in-chief, was quoted in the Indian business publication Mint as saying that [under Varadarajan's editorship] the "newsdesk was given standing instructions not to take any stories on Narendra Modi on page one". Varadrajan's resignation also triggered further drama. On 21 October, the newspaper's website explained that changes in the editorial management were due to "recurrent violations and defiance of the framework of the institution's longstanding values on the business side, and recurrent violations and defiance" of the newspaper's editorial values.

So many institutions are largely run by a single family. And the media is no exception

With Modi's popularity increasing and his profile growing, it seems Varadarajan ruffled more feathers than those of the newspaper's management. Both Ram and Ravi have denied these allegations, but Varadarajan commented in an interview on the Best Media Info website that he and his team may have trod on some "big toes". "Toes that were expecting puff pieces and not hard reporting from The Hindu. Those toes will probably be feeling relieved now," he said.

Unfortunately, the Hindu is not known to be the most harmonious board, and over the years it has had a fair few spats. There was hope that with Varadarajan, it would evolve into a more professionally run magazine. On one level, it may seem this is just another feud, and normal service will resume, but with allegations of "recurrent

violations" and the Modi issue, these signs could be a prelude to a change in tone for the newspaper.

Over the last year, some public figures have come under fire for their criticism of Modi. This is a worrying sign, a trend we are seeing being played out in every nook and cranny of the country. So as we look forward to next year's election, we hope The Hindu and the wider Indian media will put journalism ahead of politics, as India needs strong journalistic values now more than ever. ☒

© Eklavya Gupte
www.indexoncensorship.org

Eklavya Gupte is a journalist working between London and Mumbai. His articles have previously featured in the Wall Street Journal, Time Out Mumbai and The Wisden Cricketer

ABOVE: Um Radwan, a female fighter in the Free Syrian Army, stands as she holds her weapon in Aleppo's Bustan al-Basha district, October 3, 2013.

CULTURE

In this section

I write with blind eyes and forty fingers

42(4): 130/133 | DOI: 10.1177/0306422013513389

In a story written for this publication, Syrian dissident author **Samar Yazbek** reflects on what it's like to be a writer of fiction faced with the violence and atrocities of civil war and asks: how we can produce literature right now, in this era of bloodshed?

EVERYTHING IS BACK to front as I start writing my novel.

Borrowing from the four elements, I try to change the flavour of things. I squeeze all these heaped up human body parts into my fine, wiry script.

It's the novel that is writing me, not the other way round. The text and I have a strange kind of relationship: we write each other and side by side we metamorphose. This novel is one I can never end; it continues to grow inside me, or an offshoot of it, and within it I grow, too. Writers are wrong if they don't believe that they are written by their words, that it is the text that gives them form. Before we write the narrative, it writes us.

The world is spinning on its gravitational axis, stripped bare of all but its insanity. I defy this force of gravity; I pluck at the flakes of skin in the downy hair of my forearms; I drag city after city behind me. I am not a real person, I am a figment of the imagination, and I long to steep myself into the details of real life – quite the opposite of the people I write about. My characters are real, of flesh and blood: they are not the product of fiction. I alone am the one swimming in the realm of the imaginary; an idea of reality, a fantasy floating in the madness.

I write, fumbling with 40 fingers. I write with eyes that do not see.

I am not a woman possessed as I have seemed all my life. I am just a word. The text spins it into an entire lifetime, a reality which I live and write, and from which I hide. I look at the people around me as though I were one of them, a world made of paper, of beams of light gone astray. I hear the roar of the larger-than-life jet planes and I whisper to myself that these are only words, a mere detail in a written text, a short text which reads:

"She hears the thunder of the shelling and she trembles. Forcing herself to continue, she prays that the planes won't take any of the children she has just said goodbye to. She's worried the other women might notice the trembling in her eyes and hands, so she grasps their hands and together they form a circle under the colonnade of the house. 'The shelling is far away,' she says. 'No need to panic.'"

When I compose to myself in my head, I have to make myself believe that I'm a character in the narrative to start describing

ABOVE: A woman carries bread in the countryside town of Minbij City near Aleppo, Syria, 18 October 2013

the real world and the people within it. If, after another round of shelling, in the bright, sunny light of day, I discover the body of a child who has wet himself, I close my eyes and brush soil over his innocent, young corpse. I whisper to myself:

"She covers him with the heaps of dust that have fallen from the ceiling of the house, feeling the warmth that is still present in his body, a body that only a moment ago was pulsating with life. She feels the moisture on the boy's mangled trunk and looks to his waist where a damp patch seeps a dark brown into the dust."

I write with 40 fingers. I myself am far from a lifelike character. I write about the woman whose fingers tremble as she examines the flesh flayed from the child's body. I have no need to panic, because I am me – not her. And she is not me. I can lead my life as I please. I am a coward, a woman of flesh and blood. I can feel my heart pounding as the bodies are heaped up in a small truck before my eyes. We swap roles and I become nothing but a storyteller from a time

of legends, whose dreams are haunted by the *jinn* and the siren call of orphans, where the earth is sodden with the blood of young men and the rage of grieving mothers bereft of their sons. MiG fighters scatter a honeycomb of shell holes across the plateau: entrances not to Alice's Wonderland, but to a wretched inferno.

I am lost in this garden, floating through this dark underworld. I'm the only one to come from nothingness and return to the make-believe, amidst a range of characters strewn throughout the narrative from start to finish, all trapped in the blazing heat over the flames of the hellfire. I hover above – neither tumbling in, nor rising out of reach of the tongues of fire. Since we were children, life has descended into this purgatory, the flames licking and looping into nooses around our necks.

I devour my heart, swallowing it haltingly, without relish.

Onwards I walk, without a head on my shoulders. My father carries me and looks at the emptiness that was once his daughter. →

→ I lay naked stretched out on the pavement. A sniper takes his pleasure filling my body with a series of bullet holes. It was here that not long ago they threw me down and raped me. They stole my baby and I could hear his screams as they threw themselves on top of me. I carry the limbs of my children in these hands; I look up at the sky that shortly before was swarming with aircraft. I am the sky, slain in battle.

I am made by the act of writing about it. It is through these women that I take on real form. And yet, inside I am hollow.

Those long months were marked by the smell of blood in a small room under bombardment, where I crept furtively into a corner one day and secretly watched two old women sleeping alone in a house abandoned by its owners. Everyone had died in the fighting. There, in that surreptitious moment, I realised that we authors cannot possibly see writing as an ordinary act, and indeed perhaps should not even contemplate starting to write at a time like this, for to attempt it means stumbling on the threshold of madness. How is literature even possible at the moment? Like philosophy and history, the art of literature and storytelling is supposed to broaden our knowledge, endowing us with heightened sensitivity and shrewd insight. But how can we produce literature right now, in this era of bloodshed? As I watched those two old women huddled up together under the aerial assault, I wondered how much time I would need before I could return to writing fiction. Working towards a novel is the least I can do to try to document this pain. But what I write now is not fiction: I am simply revealing the many layers of hell to the light.

What simple and honest way is there to express it all? Well, perhaps that's beside the point. Right now, what's important is that while we're beheading one another, devouring each other's raw entrails, wandering headless, aimless, lost in a void, we have so far failed to realise the impact this all-engulfing collapse of humanity has had on our relationships, our friendships and our sense of the purpose of life. We have failed to grasp the scale of the slaughter, seeing it always from one perspective, one point of view. Perhaps we haven't lost everything yet, but while we lay waste to our land, heads continue to roll.

It's impossible even to conceive of writing about heads rolling under a hail of missiles from helicopters, when they have just this minute slaughtered a quiet, gentle lad who was looking after some refugee children, a harmless youngster who knew nothing more of life than how to smile and breed pigeons.

I cannot stop thinking about the old woman I lived with during the airstrikes who, when she fell into a deep coma, was taken by her sons far from the house out onto the Saraqib steppes, so that she wouldn't be killed in the shelling. Her flesh started to decay while she was still alive, and yet she didn't wake up. Her heart is still beating.

Would someone like to tell me that this is a true story? Or is it perhaps a surreal detail from a Latin American magic realist novel, so popular among Arab readers?

No, it's a real story which I've pulled out from deep within me, which I've lived, which I've smelled myself and seen with my own eyes; I can't describe it as an event from a fictional narrative. It's the story that made a woman choose silence and isolation, after seeing the political elites rip each other's organs to shreds and collapse in a vacuum of hatred, while the stars of simple souls rise to light up a world that cowers in hiding. All this has forced the writer to master the art of spinning silence and weaving pain until the last spark of life within her fades. And yet, still, she cannot write it as a novel. Is pain given living testimony through her alone? She will narrate this pain as it is, alive and all-consuming, as long as fiction can also be documentary and as long as the

author herself can carry on playing a role in the fabric of the novel.

I still haven't found my own skin. I am wandering amidst the bodies gone astray in the burnt wastelands beneath the aerial bombardment. I'm still looking for a small flicker of meaning in all of this destruction and insanity, which emerged so suddenly from the clay of the earth and rained down on us from the sky in torrents.

I can write and write and write.

Every day, I write. I know no other art but this, and there is nothing I have mastered besides immersing myself in the narrative. I write about myself as someone who lives in real life, but who is in fact only observing it. I'm not really here. I'm in another world, far away. A world not bounded by four walls of clay, the walls of a shallow grave.

I was there.

And I still am. I watch how in a flash the light of their eyes is extinguished.

I watched this woman as her trembling hands sensed the warm dampness which suddenly burst from a little girl. She embraced her, mistakenly believing she was still alive as she wet herself. In vain, the woman hoped to preserve the girl's faint heartbeat. Neither did the writer realise at first that her heart had been silenced in an instant; she had not seen the gaping black hole pierced through her chest. ⊠

Translated by Ruth Ahmedzai Kemp

www.indexoncensorship.org

Born in 1970 in Jable, Syria, Samar Yazbek studied literature before beginning her career as a journalist and a scriptwriter for Syrian television and cinema. Yazbek was an active participant in the Women Initiative Organization, dedicated to the defence of women's and children's rights. She was involved in Liberties, a centre that defends the freedom of speech for journalists in Syria. She was also the editor of Women of Syria, an electronic magazine and human rights group that focuses on women, children and community in Syria. Such issues are at the heart of her literary work, and for these reasons her books have been controversial and severely criticised by the Syrian regime. In 2011 Samar Yazbek was the first to publish an account of the Syrian uprising's first four months, In the crossfire: A Diary of the Syrian Revolution, where she carefully documented the protests and the repression, recorded valuable testimonies, and described her personal despair. In 2012, The book was awarded the PEN Pinter award in the UK and the PEN Tucholsky prize in Sweden. In 2013, the book was awarded the PEN Oxfam Novib prize in the Netherlands. It was translated into French (Buchet-Chastel), English (Haus), German (Nigel & Kimche, Hanser), Dutch (Nigh & Ditmar) and Turkish (Timas). Yazbek is also the author of the novels Clay (2004), Cinnamon (2008), The Mountain of Lilies (2008), and In her Mirrors (2010). She currently lives in Paris.

Going dark

42(4): 134/148 | DOI: 10.1177/0306422013511391

Celebrated playwright **Lucien Bourjeily** talks government censorship, the latest episode in the Lebanese battle between writers and the censors, and publishes for the first time in English an exclusive extract of his controversial play, currently banned in Lebanon

WHEN WRITER LUCIEN Bourjeily made censorship the theme of his latest play, he knew he was in for a battle. And he was right. His play about censorship ended up being banned. Not surprisingly, he thinks this decision tells its own story about Lebanon today.

"Because the censorship law in Lebanon is so vague and elusive," he says, artwork that might have received approval two years ago are "censored or banned today".

"In this climate of fear," he adds, "the military obviously becomes more present in day-to-day life, tightening security (through countless check points in almost every corner of Lebanon) and tightening their grip on freedom of expression. For the near future, I fear that we will be hearing about more bans, more censorship, and more constraints on freedom of speech in Lebanon: censorship thrives when the state feels insecure or when it makes the common mistake of correlating security and freedom of expression."

On 28 August, he was summoned to the Lebanese Censorship Bureau and told that his play, Will It Pass or Not?, could not go ahead. The play, which tackles the theme of censorship head on, poses the difficult question that any Lebanese artist who explores controversial or sensitive issues must consider. Prior to Bourjeily's encounter with the interior ministry, the play was performed on university campuses

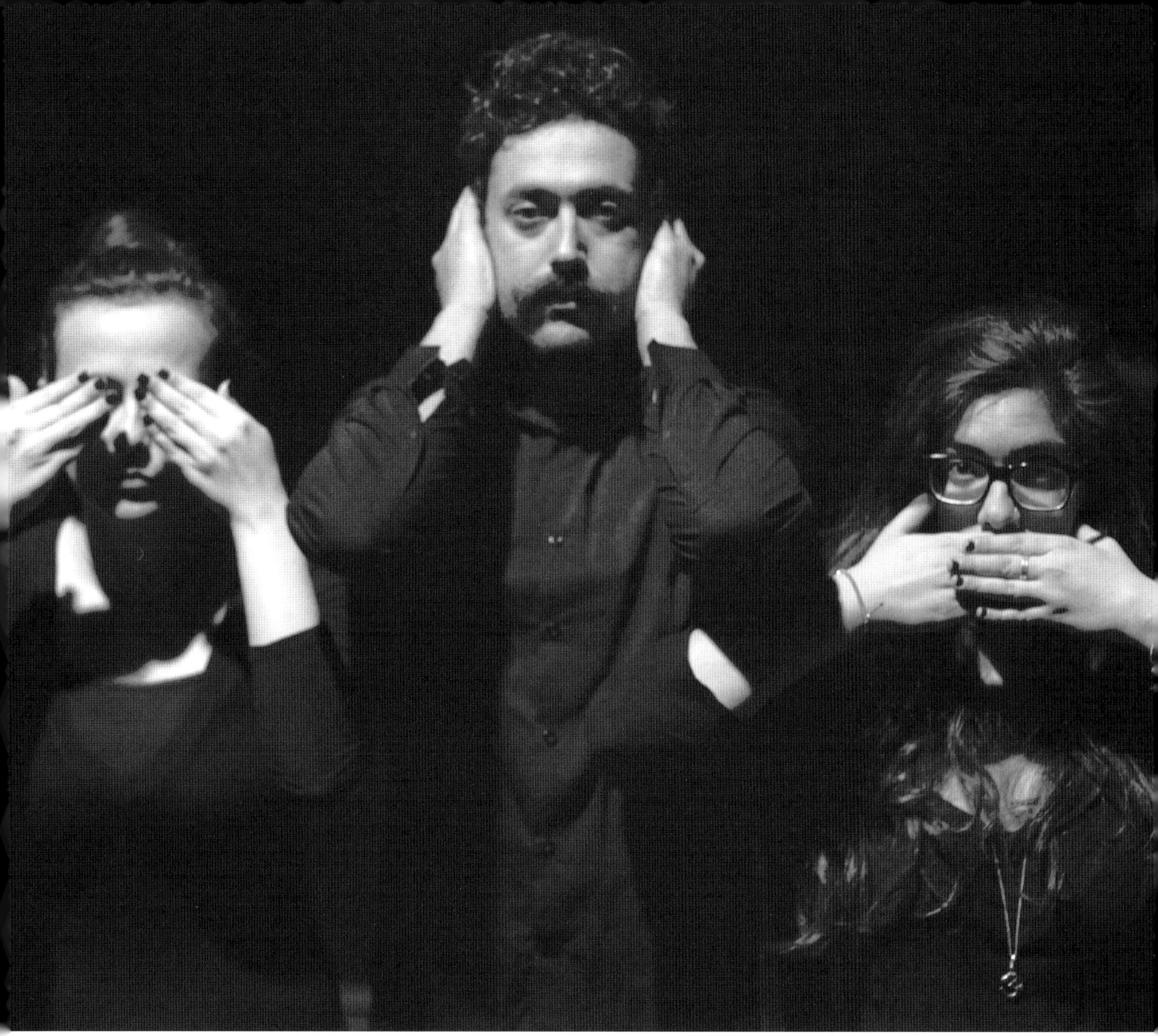

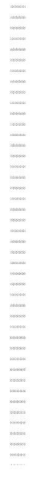

ABOVE: Publicity photograph for Will it Pass or Not?

Credit: http://www.bourjeily.com/

to invited audiences instead of theatres. Members of the censorship board attended and broke up the performance, even though a loophole in the law meant that the play could legally be performed in the venue. So Bourjeily decided to test the board and submitted the play for their consideration. On 3 September 2013, the censorship board's General Mounir Akiki appeared on television, presenting evidence from four so-called "critics" who insisted the play had no artistic merit and therefore would not be passed. Often, the board will recommend changes that will make an artistic work more palatable – a line removed, the omission of controversial material. But in this case, the play was simply rejected. Index decided to publish an extract of the play so readers could make their own minds up. →

→ In this extract from Will It Pass or Not?, below, Bourjeily exposes the ridiculousness – and arbitrary nature – of the Lebanese Censorship Bureau, which commonly bans material that is deemed to be obscene, offensive to religions or politically sensitive.

Scene 2

Sergeant Da'ja, 35, is at his desk, looking through some papers. Kareem, 27, a director, is sitting on a chair next to the desk

Kareem raises his hand.

SERGEANT DA'JA How long have you been waiting?

KAREEM About an hour.

SERGEANT DA'JA What have you got?

KAREEM A screenplay.

SERGEANT DA'JA Go on then, show me.

KAREEM Please, here you are.

Kareem passes Da'ja the screenplay.

SERGEANT DA'JA You've been here before, haven't you?

KAREEM Yes, I submitted a request, but it just got sent back. Someone from your office contacted me.

SERGEANT DA'JA Okay. But I can't do anything with it. Revisions are done by Captain Shadid.

KAREEM Can I see Captain Shadid?

SERGEANT DA'JA When the Captain is willing to see you. You'll have to wait.

KAREEM I'll wait.

Captain Shadid, 40, enters the room. Da'ja stands to attention.

SERGEANT DA'JA Good day to you, sir.

Flustered, Da'ja shuffles his papers. Kareem raises his hand again but Da'ja ignores him. Da'ja enters the Captain's office, stamps his foot on the ground and gives a military salute.

CAPTAIN SHADID What have we got today, then?

SERGEANT DA'JA The Sun newspaper, as usual, sir.

We need censorship. What would life be like without any kind of oversight? It'd be carnage

Da'ja hands the newspaper to the captain.

CAPTAIN SHADID Madame Noha again, I suppose…

SERGEANT DA'JA As usual, sir.

CAPTAIN SHADID Have you even read it, you little shit? No, no, no… Just the same old rubbish. Goodness me … What am I to do with her?

SERGEANT DA'JA You know best, sir.

CAPTAIN SHADID Okay, what else have we got today? Are there many waiting out there?

SERGEANT DA'JA There's someone outside who'd like to speak to you … about his film script. It's the tedious one about sectarianism in →

→ Lebanon and the guys who go to India and set up a secular state … and all that nonsense.

CAPTAIN SHADID Yes, yes, I remember. Show him in …

SERGEANT DA'JA: Yes, sir.

Da'ja stamps his feet and salutes, then leaves the room.

Captain Shadid makes a phone call.

CAPTAIN SHADID Hi, Noha. Where are you? Come in to my office, please. I'd like a word.

Da'ja goes back to writing on his papers. Kareem raises his hand again.

SERGEANT DA'JA Again? You're an inquisitive type, aren't you? Always asking questions... Okay, you can go in now.

Kareem enters Captain Shadid's office. Captain Shadid is on the phone. He gestures to Kareem to give him the screenplay and then sit down.

SERGEANT DA'JA Hello, sir. Er, one thing, sir. About your son?

CAPTAIN SHADID Yes, what about him?

SERGEANT DA'JA There's a match at 4pm today. Barcelona–Madrid. Who's going to take him?

CAPTAIN SHADID Isn't there anyone here? Isn't Sobhi here?

SERGEANT DA'JA Yes, Sobhi's here.

CAPTAIN SHADID Well, send Sobhi then.

SERGEANT DA'JA Yes, sir. Right you are, sir.

CAPTAIN SHADID Mr Kareem.

KAREEM Yes, captain?

CAPTAIN SHADID Is this your first film?

KAREEM It's the first one I've decided to film, yes. It's taken me three years to write the script.

CAPTAIN SHADID Three years and this is what you've got to show for yourself?

KAREEM It means a lot to me. What do you mean by "this"?

CAPTAIN SHADID Listen, there's something I want to tell you. I'm saying this to you like a brother to a brother. So, this film of yours … I'm afraid it just isn't up to scratch. The script was 120 pages. But we've had to do quite a lot of work on it and it's got a bit shorter … But it's turned out great.

Let's take the title, to start with … I mean, how dare you use a name like that? Fucked Up until Judgment Day? Did you really think that was acceptable? Really? Where did you get that idea?

And then there's the swearing … We counted it all up: you've got "fuck you" four times and "you son of a bitch" 14 times. I mean, do you really think that's reasonable?

KAREEM It's meant to show this guy's personality: he talks a lot of crap. It's "dramatic tension"… it's meant to reflect real life. People do speak like that in real life, captain.

CAPTAIN SHADID Lots of people do all kinds of things but it doesn't mean it gets our approval, my dear man. We really couldn't condone this character … so we've cut him out altogether. Dramatic tension or not: there were quite a few other things we've had to cut out too … Like the first scene, for example. So these guys storm out of their sectarian community and stand up to the cleric. You show the priest getting up to mischief and the sheikh taking bribes.

And these guys who just run away, off to India … We can't have it like this. We've got to think of our country's image, too. So →

ABOVE: Lucien Bourjeily

→ we've cut out that whole scene. But don't worry – we'll replace it with another scene with the same ending … The guys can leave the country, that's fine … and go to India … but for tourism instead. So we're just changing the mood a bit. The film's much nicer this way. Better to have a film showing a nice, pleasant world rather than this ugly nightmare you had originally. Tourists are great, so the whole idea is much nicer than the stuff with the clerics and the corruption and the bribes … And at the same time, this will encourage tourism: after all, Lebanon is a superb touristic destination.

KAREEM But now the film has lost its entire meaning!

CAPTAIN SHADID What do you mean it's lost its meaning? It's got even more meaning now! Listen, we're a country of diversity, of coexistence … Your film was very inflammatory. It made the country look like a well of sectarian conflict, where clerics are stirring up trouble and exploiting the country's problems for their own political motives … No, no, no – we can't have that.

KAREEM But, sir, how can we solve our country's problems if we don't talk about them?

CAPTAIN SHADID Ha, ha, ha, ha, ha, ha … Ah, so you want to solve the country's problems now, do you? With your film? Ah, that's wonderful … Ha, ha, ha …

Listen, I've got to uphold the law. There are certain parameters I have to work within. And the second scene, where they arrive in India and meet the Indian cleric … well, if he's portrayed in a negative light, then – even if he's Indian – it reflects negatively on Lebanese clerics, too. No, no, no – we can't allow that. Why don't we have him meeting someone else, instead – a salesman, perhaps? Something useful like that … The Lebanese are renowned for their business acumen, after all, and this would fit with the tourism angle. We've killed two birds with one stone … and made it all much simpler. This way, we can approve the text … As for the third scene [he looks down at the screenplay], well … I don't really think the film needs to be 120 pages long. So, now we've got it down to 20 pages. It's great… Better than nothing, anyway, so roll with it!

KAREEM But, sir, now it's just a short film!

CAPTAIN SHADID Yes, but why not? My niece made a lovely short film and it was a big hit at all the festivals round the world. What do you have against short films?

KAREEM Sir, it's just… [Gets a bit flustered] … It's just I … I don't understand how you've got it down to 20 pages!

CAPTAIN SHADID Khalas, come now – no need to get all hot and bothered. Honestly, I get hundreds of scripts on my desk every day and I assure you, your screenplay is much better this way. It'd make a lovely short film. God grant you success!

KAREEM But, Captain Shadid, I've spent three years working on this script! Can't we come to a compromise? Can't we see if there are any smaller changes we could make instead?

CAPTAIN SHADID [answering the telephone] Hello? Yes, Brigadier-General. Certainly, sir. Yes, sir. I'm looking into the matter right now, sir.

Captain Shadid gestures to Kareem to see himself out of his office. Kareem leaves the room and sits down on a chair in Sergeant Da'ja's office. Da'ja enters.

Kareem raises his hand again.

SERGEANT DA'JA What, are you still here?

* * *

→

→ ### Scene 5

Noha enters Captain Shadid's office.

CAPTAIN SHADID Hi.

NOHA Are you angry?

CAPTAIN SHADID Me? Why would I be angry? My wife criticises my job day in day out... and today she's gone as far as mentioning me by name! What did you have to go and put my name in for? Why?

NOHA Darling, you're the one who's forbidden her from putting on the play.

CAPTAIN SHADID What do you mean forbidden?

NOHA Well, what else am I supposed to say?

CAPTAIN SHADID Hmmm ... So ... What, have you been to see this play, then?

NOHA Of course. But I doubt you have?

CAPTAIN SHADID She gets naked in it!

NOHA What makes you say that? Have you even seen it?

CAPTAIN SHADID No, I've not been to see it... But I've heard plenty about it from the others. What difference does it make if I've seen it? It contains nudity! But, anyway, nudity or not... you shouldn't be meddling in my work!

NOHA I'm just doing the same with my work as you do with yours. As a journalist, I just express my opinion about things... and then you go and meddle in my work.

CAPTAIN SHADID My job is to enforce the law.

NOHA Yes, and who wrote that law?

CAPTAIN SHADID Who wrote the law? Who? The law is in the name of the Lebanese people!

NOHA What, so don't you think the Lebanese people want to go to see this play? Because there's never an empty seat in the theatre whenever I go.

CAPTAIN SHADID Listen, I'm just doing my job... What do you want me to do? I'm your husband... So? What do you want from me? You want me to abolish censorship? Shut down the entire directorate? Sit at home and twiddle my thumbs? Give 200 soldiers the boot?

NOHA Yeah, yeah, very funny.

CAPTAIN SHADID Well, it's just not acceptable. Every day, it's the same old story with you. Isn't there anything else in the country you could write about besides me?

NOHA I'm not the first to write about politics and have you censor it! You're always saying, "Give it up, girl. You're just banging your head against a brick wall." Well, what else should I write about? First, no politics... and now art is banned as well. What should I write about, then? I may as well throw in the towel and sit at home. Is that what you'd rather? You're always trying to censor me just like those naked women that pile up on your desk.

CAPTAIN SHADID Well, we need censorship. What would life be like without any kind of oversight? It'd be carnage... Are we back in the dark ages living in a forest? Children need oversight, society needs oversight.

NOHA You said it! Children need oversight – but we're not children! I'm not a child and I want to see the plays I want to see... Man, living in a forest in the dark ages would be better than living with you.　　　　　　　　　　　　　　　→

ABOVE: Publicity photograph for Will It Pass or Not?

→ **CAPTAIN SHADID** What do you want? Shall I get your editor to censor you or shall I pull the plug on your magazine? I mean it... Do you understand?

NOHA Go ahead, then, censor it. Who's going to rush out and buy it, anyway? You guys think it's just "oversight"... but it's not – it's propaganda. And forbidding things just makes them more desirable.

CAPTAIN SHADID All right, enough. But just watch it, you. I can always divorce you!

Kareem is still waiting in Sergeant's Da'ja's office

Credit: http://www.bourjeily.com

SERGEANT DA'JA So, your name's Dalloum? Where are you from?

KAREEM The Beqaa Valley.

SERGEANT DA'JA Ah, Brigadier-General Dalloum is from Beqaa. Brigadier-General Damian Dalloum.

KAREEM Damian Dalloum's a great guy.

SERGEANT DA'JA You know him?

KAREEM He's my father's cousin.

SERGEANT DA'JA Wallahi, no way! His cousin? His cousin? Gosh. Wait here a minute.

*Da'ja enters the **Captain**'s office, stamps his foot on the ground and gives a military salute.*

SERGEANT DA'JA Er, excuse me, sir. The chap who's just been in to see you this morning about the Indian film … from the Dalloum family.

CAPTAIN SHADID Yes, that's all dealt with.

SERGEANT DA'JA Yes, but he's still here waiting … We've just been talking and it turns out that he's a Dalloum Dalloum … He's related to Brigadier-General Dalloum!

CAPTAIN SHADID Damian Dalloum?

SERGEANT DA'JA Yes, sir…

CAPTAIN SHADID Well, why didn't he say so?

SERGEANT DA'JA I don't know, sir, I don't think he realised.

CAPTAIN SHADID What do you mean – he didn't realise?

→ **SERGEANT DA'JA** He didn't realise that Brigadier-General Dalloum worked here in the directorate.

CAPTAIN SHADID How could he not know?

SERGEANT DA'JA He might not have known. What would you like to do, sir?

CAPTAIN SHADID This film … we've had a look at it, right?

SERGEANT DA'JA Yes … it's a bit disrespectful in places, with some swearing … and the title's rather strange …

CAPTAIN SHADID The film's fine.

SERGEANT DA'JA Yes, sir, there's not really much to say about it.

CAPTAIN SHADID We could perhaps just change the title.

SERGEANT DA'JA But it's fine, otherwise.

CAPTAIN SHADID Yes, yes. What are you doing waiting out there? Show him in.

SERGEANT DA'JA Yes, sir.

Da'ja steps back to his own office

SERGEANT DA'JA The captain would like to see you.

Kareem stands up and enters Captain Shadid's office

CAPTAIN SHADID Come in, Dalloum. Please, sit down. This is my wife, Noha. She writes for the Sun newspaper.

KAREEM A pleasure to meet you. I always read your paper.

CAPTAIN SHADID Mr Kareem, your film is wonderful.

KAREEM The short or the long version?

CAPTAIN SHADID No, the long version, of course! It's a great film, wonderful!

KAREEM But weren't there a few things …?

CAPTAIN SHADID No, no. We've just gone back and had another look, and you were right: there's not really anything to worry about. It's very realistic, after all, and it's got just the right amount of social and political criticism.

KAREEM You mean, you'll give me permission to film it?

CAPTAIN SHADID Yes, yes, of course. Don't you fret! [To Noha] This film gets our full approval. You see: if it's a great work of art, we approve it, and if it's not, we don't. It's simple. Why do you always have to make such a mountain out of a molehill?

CAPTAIN SHADID God bless you, Mr Kareem. Go and see Sergeant Da'ja and he'll sign it off.

KAREEM Yes, captain. Thank you very much, sir!

SERGEANT DA'JA Wallahi! So the captain has given you the go ahead?

Kareem steps back into Sergeant Da'ja's office.

KAREEM Yes, er …

SERGEANT DA'JA He hasn't changed the title?

KAREEM No, it's as it was.

SERGEANT DA'JA It's a wonderful film, very deep. It made a great impression on us all. I was the one who suggested that the captain had another look. So, I'll just sign it off, and then →

→ you come back tomorrow for the permit – if it's not too much trouble?

KAREEM Not at all. It's no trouble.

SERGEANT DA'JA And Brigadier-General Dalloum will be here tomorrow too, so you can say hello. I'll take you to see him. So, please, mind how you go. And what else have I forgotten? Ah yes, here's my phone number, just in case.

KAREEM Your number?

SERGEANT DA'JA Yes, come to me direct, if there's anything at all you need! ☒

Translated by Ruth Ahmedzai Kemp

Director and filmmaker Lucien Bourjeily brought interactive, improvised theatre to Lebanese audiences, introducing the first improvisational theatre troupe, ImproBeirut, to the Middle East in 2008. His hard-hitting play 66 Minutes in Damascus, which draws on journalists' and activists' descriptions of Syrian detention centres, showcased at the London International Festival of Theatre in summer 2012, receiving critical acclaim. With Kiki Bokassa, he is the co-founder of the Visual and Performing Arts Association, which advocates the use of creative arts to help resolve social issues. Bourjeily is the winner of the 2009 British Council's Young Creative Entrepreneur Award; he won the title of best director at the 2008 Beirut International Film Festival for his debut film Taht El Aaricha; and was awarded a Fulbright Scholarship in 2010, graduating with a Master in Fine Arts in Film from Loyola Marymount University (Los Angeles). He is also the author of Index on Censorship's Tripwires manual.

©Lucien Borjeily
www.indexoncensorship.org

Coercion and warnings

42(4): 149/152 | DOI: 10.1177/0306422013511400

Qatari poet **Mohammed al Ajami Ibn al Dhib** is in prison for what he has expressed in his poetry. Index translates this poem, inspired by the Tunisian revolution, into English for the first time

Jasmine Revolution

Prime minister Mohamed al Ghannouchi:
If we measured your might
it wouldn't hold a candle
to a constitution.
We shed no tears for Ben Ali,
nor any for his rule.
It was nothing more than an interlude for us,
historical and dictatorial,
a system of oppression,
an era of autocracy.
Tunisia proclaimed the people's revolt:
When we lay blame
only the base and vile feel it;
and when we praise
we do so with all our hearts.
A revolution was kindled with the blood of the people:
Their glory had worn away,
the glory of every living soul.
So, rebel, tell them,
tell them in a shrouded voice, a voice from the grave:
Tell them that tragedies precede all victories.
A warning to the country whose ruler is ignorant,
whose ruler deems that power

ABOVE: A view of Doha's business district, Qatar

→   comes from the American army.
A warning to the country
whose people starve
while the regime boasts of its prosperity.
A warning to the country whose citizens sleep:
One moment you have your rights,
the next they're taken from you.
A warning to the system – inherited – of oppression.
How long have all of you been slaves
to one man's selfish predilections?
How long will the people remain
ignorant of their own strength,
while a despot makes decrees and appointments,
the will of the people all but forgotten?
Why is it that a ruler's decisions are carried out?
They'll come back to haunt him
in a country willing
to rid itself of coercion.

Let him know, he
who pleases only himself, and does nothing
but vex his own people; let him know
that tomorrow
someone else will be seated on that throne,
someone who knows the nation is not his own,
nor the property of his children.
It belongs to the people, and its glories
are the glories of the people.
They gave their reply, and their voice was one,
and their fate, too, was one.
All of us are Tunisia
in the face of these oppressors.
The Arab regimes and those who rule them
are all, without exception,
without a single exception,
shameful, thieves.
This question that keeps you up at night –
its answer won't be found
on any of the official channels…
Why, why do these regimes
import everything from the West –
everything but the rule of law, that is,
and everything but freedom?

Translated by Kareem James Abu-Zeid
© Mohammed al Ajami Ibn al Dhib

→

→ Mohammed al Ajami Ibn al Dhib was born in Qatar. A father of four, he spent three years studying Arabic literature at Cairo University. While he was there, in August 2010, he held a private poetry recital in his flat. A member of the audience recorded it on camera and uploaded a video of him reciting Jasmine Revolution to the internet.

More than a year later, al Ajami was arrested in Doha, Qatar, and charged with insulting Sheikh Hamad bin Khalifa al Thani, Emir of Qatar from 1995 until his abdication in 2013, and "incitement to overthrow the ruling system". The latter offence may be punishable by death.

In November 2012, after months of incarceration in solitary confinement, he was found guilty and sentenced to life imprisonment (later reduced to 15 years). Al Ajami, 37, has always acknowledged his authorship of the poem but has denied that he ever intended it to be insulting towards the emir. ☒

Index around the world

by **Mike Harris**

INDEX NEWS

42(4): 153/154 | DOI: 10.1177/0306422013513113

NEXT YEAR IT will be 25 years since the fall of the Berlin Wall, a seminal moment for free speech in Europe. For the collapse of Communism did not just mark the end of the Soviet Union's brutal regimes in Europe, with their censorship boards, all-encompassing state surveillance and imprisonment of dissident voices (all captured and chronicled by Index on Censorship); it opened up an opportunity for Europe to reunite after 45 years of division.

Index on Censorship's recently published report on freedom of expression in the European Union looked at how the EU and its member states are dealing with free speech, both domestically and in their foreign policies. It's a complex picture. For central and Eastern Europe, there can be no doubt that enlargement has played a hugely positive role in improving respect for human rights, but this transition has been patchy. While the Baltic states are attempting to become beacons for internet freedom, Hungary has slipped backwards, with a clampdown on press freedom and new restrictions on whistleblowers. Freedom of expression also remains an issue in countries that joined the EU in its early days. Many of these still criminalise defamation, particularly that directed at politicians and heads of state. The report shows how important is to for the EU to do more to ensure that its member states remain true to the values that inspired the union.

The fall of the Berlin Wall left many behind. While the collapse of the Soviet Union freed a number of European states, others found that one repressive political system was replaced by another.

Azerbaijan is ruled by the corrupt Aliyev dynasty, a family feted by high society in London and Paris, but whose government blackmails and uses violence against journalists and activists. Index visited Baku in October to see the situation at first hand in the run-up to the country's presidential election. Ilham Aliyev took office in 2003. Since then there has not been a single fair election. Our delegation was hassled by security officers as they attempted to take photos, and the journalists and human rights defenders they spoke to live in fear of violence, physical and psychological threats and the use of libel. The authorities fail to investigate the murder of and violence against journalists, which creates an atmosphere of impunity and encourages further attacks. NGOs that promote freedom of expression are shut down or their work is investigated by the authorities. Index's report "Locking up free expression" details these violations and paints a grim picture of a country in which the conditions for free expression are →

→ deteriorating. Yet Azerbaijan has its vocal supporters – British MPs Mike Hancock and Robert Walter travelled there to monitor the election and said they did not witness electoral violations. But in a country where there is no free independent television, where the main opposition's candidate was barred from standing for election at the last minute, and where youth activists are detained and beaten up, how free can these elections possibly be?

Index has also been closely involved in freedom of expression battles in the UK, where we have focused on follow-up to the Leveson Inquiry and on mass surveillance.

The EU is yet to develop a coherent digital strategy. With digital freedom now a major public concern, it is clearly time to do so

Cross-party support in British politics is a rare thing indeed, but the political response to the Leveson Inquiry has seen politicians line up in favour of a regulatory body for press regulation that is backed by statute. This worrying unanimity in favour of press regulation has led to an unacceptable level of political interference in the workings of a free press. Index remains concerned that the waving through of the Royal Charter has destroyed any hopes of the tough independent self-regulation that will ensure the protection of free speech in the UK. In particular, significant concerns remain over what the Leveson requirements will mean for whistleblowers.

In August, British police arrested David Miranda, the partner of the jounalist behind many of the reports on Edward Snowden's revelations about the National Security Agency's and the UK Government Communications Headquarters's mass surveillance of the internet. British police detained Miranda under anti-terror legislation and destroyed computers owned by the Guardian newspaper, both troubling signs of how fragile press freedom is. Index's petition calling for the EU heads of state and government to state their opposition to all systems of mass surveillance was signed by nearly 7,000 people from across Europe. Celebrities such as broadcaster Stephen Fry and artist Anish Kapoor spoke out in favour of our campaign alongside 40 NGOs from across the world. We wait to see if our call for this issue to take centre stage during the European Council Summit has been heeded. After initial prevarication, the issue is becoming increasingly politically charged, with France and Brazil speaking out against US surveillance of its own citizens and the Snowden revelations becoming the number two political issue during the recent German elections. Yet without concerted action, it seems that little will change. Building systems of mass surveillance undercover is perhaps easier than dismantling them once discovered. As Index has pointed out before, the EU is yet to develop a coherent digital strategy. With digital freedom now a major public concern, it is clearly time to do so.

Twenty-five years after the fall of the Berlin Wall, a lot remains to be done across Europe and beyond to guarantee free speech. The values we hoped the EU and its member states would champion remain in flux. We must redouble our efforts. ☒

www.indexoncensorship.org

Mike Harris is head of advocacy at Index on Censorship

Words count

END NOTE

42(4): 155/156 | DOI: 10.1177/0306422013512971

Most schools try to get their pupils to be creative with their language. But when they go in the opposite direction and start banning words, they are helping neither the students or themselves, says **Milana Knezevic**

EVERY NOW AND then you reach a certain milestone that makes you realise you've grown up a bit. Like moving away from home, graduating and getting your first real job. There's also the moment when it hits you that you don't seem to speak the same language as younger people. This happened to me a while ago. The scene: an Index on Censorship youth event. The topic: social media. In a heated group discussion, someone mentioned the word "preing". Cue blank stares from most people over the age of 20. It was promptly explained that it means looking up people on Facebook before meeting them. This practice is not unknown to my generation (teenagers ourselves not all that long ago), but we stopped short of giving it a word of its own. If we're struggling to keep up with the seemingly ever-changing slang of today, I can see how others might think it easiest to ban it all.

And some have tried to do just that. The Harris Academy in Upper Norwood, London recently produced a list of words and phrases students were banned from using. It included "like", "bare" and "innit", as well as starting sentences with "basically" and finishing them with "yeah". This isn't the only example in recent times of schools taking steps against language that, for whatever reason, is deemed inappropriate. Earlier this year, Sacred Heart Primary School in Middlesbrough wrote to parents asking them to monitor their children's use of regional phrases like "yous" and "it's nowt".

Both schools argued they were only trying to give their students a leg-up on the future career ladder. A Harris Academy spokesperson said the ban would help students "to develop the soft skills they will need to compete for jobs and university places". "I don't want the children to be disadvantaged. Using standard English in applications and job interviews is important," explained Sacred Heart head teacher Carol Walker.

I am certain they do believe they are acting in the kids' best interest, and this is perhaps not the most pressing issue on the freedom of expression agenda. You might be disappointed, but not surprised, to learn that Index isn't currently planning a campaign in support of the oppressed students of Croydon and Teesside. But we do tend to subscribe to the view that banning words generally is not the solution to your problems.

First of all, if certain words are popular and prevalent enough for people to decide that a ban is needed to purge them from people's vocabulary, I would venture to →

→ say the ban probably won't work. Add to this the truth generally acknowledged that if you tell a kid they can't do something, chances are they will want to do it more, and the whole idea starts to seem quite silly.

Besides, one of the most beautiful things about language is that it's dynamic and constantly evolving. There was a time when

If we're struggling to keep up with the seemingly ever-changing slang of today, I can see how others might think it easiest to ban it all

"cool" was considered slang, and if used in a job interview might very well have prevented you getting a call-back. Then there's "ace", "chuffed", "hang out", "dig", "made up about it", "dis" and hundreds of other words and phrases that could have featured on lists of banned slang and/or regional phrases in years gone by. Who's to say that in 2023 you won't get a round of applause in the boardroom for a "bare informative presentation"? X

www.indexoncensorship.org

Milana Knezevic is editorial assistant at Index on Censorship